AF590051

The Year of Champions

The Story of the 2011 Collinsville High School Marching Band

Kaitlyn Auer

The Year of Champions
The Story of the 2011 Collinsville High School Marching Band
Kaitlyn Auer

Copyright © 2013 Kaitlyn Auer

All rights reserved. No part of this publication may be reproduced, distributed, or transmitted in any form or by any means, or stored in a database or retrieval system, without the prior written permission of the author.

ISBN: 978-1-300-85996-3

Printed in the United States of America

Cover design by Mathew Votoupal
Photos used with permission of Mathew Votoupal

First Edition: April 2013

10 9 8 7 6 5 4 3 2 1

To Mr. Joseph Padawan, former director of the Collinsville High School Band Program, for rescuing the program and starting us off on the right foot

AND

To Mr. Robert Wright, for picking up where he left off and giving our band program a bright future.

Table of Contents

Introduction

It all started with a bet.

I was a couch potato intent on enjoying the summer in an air-conditioned house. My younger brother, Zach, told me he thought I couldn't survive a season of marching band. To prove him wrong, I signed up for marching band.

At first, everything seemed ordinary, except our band director's expectations for us.

And then everything changed.

Our band was like any other. It was small for our school size. The marching band had fewer than seventy members, and we had one band director, one guard instructor, and one drum instructor, plus a few techs.

We were just like any other band. We lived and breathed band. There were the obsessed-with-band kids, the crazy ones, the over-achievers, and the funny ones.

What happened in the course of one season inspired me to write this book. We did things we had never done before, pushed ourselves harder than ever before, and created a new legacy for our previously undistinguished marching program as the Champions of Collinsville High School.

We are the Collinsville High School Marching Band from Collinsville, Illinois, home of the Kahoks and the High School of Champions.

This is our story.

-Kaitlyn Auer

Part 1: Sunrise

Chapter 1: The Sun

The concrete baked beneath the sun on July 25, 2011, a humid Monday morning, at 8:35 a.m. The sun was high, and the temperature was prematurely in the upper nineties. The grass- what little of it there was in the practice field between the cafeteria and main building- scorched. Bees coasted lazily from budding weed to weed, humming incongruously with the chirp of the birds and the deafening cry of the cicadas.

Few of the students had yet arrived at the high school. The three drum majors- Kayla Kroder, head drum major, Molly McClelland and Staci Turck, assistant drum majors- were already in the Collinsville High School band room. Several other members, the majority being section leaders, started to appear. Dominick Viviano, the tremendous concert trombone player, pulled up in his enormous black diesel truck. John Bailey, trumpet section leader and Horn Sergeant, arrived on his bike. The mellophones (a marching version of the french horn) arrived shortly after their leader, Jordan Olive, who was checking the sound cart for battery and preparing to fetch the lift (a cherry-picker used to run rehearsal).

By 8:50 most of the students had trickled in, amounting to a group of about sixty-five members, including woodwinds, brass, drum line (battery), and pit assembled in the band room. The freshmen hopped around excitedly, chatting and laughing with their friends as they adjusted to their new habitat of two weeks. Aside from the freshmen, there were several older students new to marching band this year, including two flute players, myself and a sophomore, Rachel Harty, among various others. The seasoned veterans talked quietly among themselves; the freshmen were anxious fireballs shooting from one end of the band room to the other.

That habitat, the Collinsville High School band room, was a spacious room with locker shelves lining half of the walls, one wall of mirrors in the back, and a trophy wall with an interior window and door leading to the band office. The room had a short gray-brown Berber carpet with soda stains lurking inconspicuously in the whimsical pattern and a high roof that drowned out our music when it rained. Currently, band lockers were all open and cases and backpacks were strewn about across the floor. There were no chairs in the room.

When the clock, which was propped up on the top of one of the lockers, passed 9:05, the leadership team of drum majors and section leaders strolled in. Slowly the room grew still; the cacophony of squeals and growls from the woodwinds and low brass, the whinnying of the trumpets, and the buzzing of the saxophones ceased.

Sun streamed through the lofty window blinds and warmed the bandroom. Silence enveloped the anxious students.

I, like many others, had been told gruesome and graphic details of our sport. My younger brother, now a sophomore, said this: "Katy, you won't survive a *day* in marching band. We actually go *outside*." Last year, he showed me each new shiny blister from marching baritone. He told of kids getting sun poisoning and passing out. I cringed each day in concert band last year when I saw countless fellow band members walk in resembling lobsters from head to toe. Drinking milk any time before eight at night was a *huge* mistake, and forgetting water could make life a nightmare of suffering for eleven hours.

We made a bet, my brother and I, whether or not I

could survive marching band. It wasn't really me accepting the bet- my common sense would have urged me to enjoy the air-conditioned summer I was accustomed to, playing computer or reading in the basement. Truthfully, it was a stubborn desire to beat Zach at something and satisfy my curiosity that caused me to march my feet into the band director's office that fateful day and blurt out, "I'm doing marching band."

Few of the freshmen around me had older siblings in band. Many weren't athletic and most had nothing to do with sports. What brought us here was our love of music, performance, and each other. A musician can be capable of playing a difficult symphony, but without the accompaniment of fellow musicians, plays only a solo.

The podium sitting in front of the director's desk and projector screen was gray and currently empty. As the section leaders began to corral unruly members into a dense cluster at the center of the room, the drum line filtered in, drums and all. The color guard walked in holding only pocket-sized notebooks, leaving their flags still rolled and zipped into their travel pouches.

And then Joseph Padawan walked in.

Mr. Padawan, or simply "Padawan" to most students, was the young director for the past two years at Collinsville- two years, granted, in which Collinsville had begun to place in competitions. A short-notice arrangement left Collinsville without a band director in the middle of the summer in 2009, when band directors were already locked into contracts. Several interviews fell through for both the high school and the middle school positions. Time was growing short to fill both positions before school started, and both the Intermediate School (fifth and sixth grades) band director, Mr. Van, and the band parents were extremely anxious. Mr. Van took care of the high school parade practices so the local parades would have their beloved music features. His wife, a talented flute player, taught the middle-school kids.

Three days before school started band directors were hired for each school. We had a name, and we had little expectation; the students anticipated meeting the new directors eagerly. The concert bands for the high school were squared, but the marching band was in a tough corner. There had been no marching camp -a traditional necessity- no music picked out, and to top it off, a new director that we would have to warm up to.

Someone smiled upon our program; where we might have acquired a teacher who knew little of marching band, or cared little about one of the programs or the other, we were sent Mr. Padawan.

I was a freshman, one of the first students to meet our new director on the first day of school.

Mr. Padawan was unlike anything we imagined. Young and fresh out of college, he performed in various bands and was a staff member for the Carolina Crown Drum Corps brass section. He brought an incredible work ethic and inspiring determination; he was taking the helm of a careening ship as the replacement of two captains and would run not only the marching band, but also both the Symphonic Band and the prestigious Wind Ensemble- the package deal that spoiled the opportunity for other applicants.

What we were given in what seemed to be a stroke of luck to simply have a band director became something so much more valuable. We had a no-nonsense (during rehearsal), motivated teacher with a fearless attitude towards challenges. Looking back, we wouldn't have lasted without him, as a group of musicians, or our "band family," as we call it.

Now in the third year of his teaching, he was well respected and appreciated by most of his students. There were those who had their disagreements; but overall, we were strong and united.

If a pin had dropped, it would have been heard as Mr. Padawan took his place among us, forgoing the formality of the podium and instead, directed us to form a circle, taking the center as we shuffled around.

He greeted us with a typically Padawan speech; he told us first how happy he was to see us and how excited he was for this year, which was obviously true. Mr. Padawan- when starting a season of concert, marching, or even jazz band- looked forward from the very beginning of the season to every moment of the journey ahead. Motivation was a key ingredient in all our endeavors.

We were then informed of the challenge we faced. He emphasized that, "it would be like nothing you have been asked to do before." Excitement and enthusiasm swept through the room with the hopeful rays of sun peeping through the blinds. However, the air was tainted with an apprehensive fear.

I won't lie; it was a terrifying thought as a non-performer to imagine marching on a field in front of an audience marching forward, backward, and sideways holding an instrument, playing a full-length marching show from memory, without looking at the yard lines. We knew very well that professional performers made this look easy… but could a small percentage of seasoned participants and a rag-tag group of freshmen (and Rachel and I) pull off a show, let alone win anything for our efforts? Would we even survive a month of this allegedly exhausting, difficult practice?

Very few of the freshmen were involved in sports. The two long weeks of band camp we would endure would put us to the test of our limits, our capabilities, and the strength of willpower.

"Every morning, you will be expected to be outside for warm-up – led by John Bailey, our horn sergeant- and you will be expected to have decent shoes with arch support for running and marching, a black towel big enough for your instrument so we don't wreck our horns, a black binder with your music in sheet protectors, a pencil, and your dot book."

What on earth is a dot book?

A dot book, which is a small notebook with either note cards or lined pages about the size of a hand, was where we wrote information about where we moved on the field. It was essentially our lifeline during practice from the very beginning when learning the show to the last practice during "cleanup" to finish the preparation for competition. It was called a dot book because we wrote in our *dots*, or coordinates on the field.

To those unfamiliar with the field, a standard football field has two numbered sides, with the fifty-yard line in the middle. On either side, there are lines every five yards and numbered lines every ten yards, all the way to the goal line. These two sides, left and right (facing the field), we refer to as side one and side two for clarity. As performers, it is reversed for us, so when we stand facing the audience in the bleachers, our right is side one and our left is side two.

This is only half of the information we kept in our dot books. We wrote in these sides translated to "one and two" to eliminate confusion and make learning the drill easier, allowing us to be able to look up our spot if we got lost during practice.

The other information we kept was the front-to-back count. On the field the very front line (out of bounds in the game) is the Front Side Line. The second major line parallel to the front is the Front Hash. The next line is the Back Hash, and the last is the Back Side Line. An example of a front-to-back position would be "four behind the FH" (front hash). Together with side-to-side, a member's dot might be "four behind the FH, three inside the forty-five." (Closer to the fifty is inside, farther away is *outside*, measured in steps).

The whole system works like an X-Y coordinates grid. Your point on the grid is your *dot* (hence the name "dot book") and is assigned by letter and number according to rank in your section.

We soon learned what we would be doing until lunch.

"All right. Starting with flutes, in half an hour you will come in individually and audition. Play the section assigned from your music standing still, march forward eight, backward eight three times, and play your lip slurs on the move. After the flutes, the order will be clarinets, saxophones, mellos, trumpets, baritones, and tubas. Break!"

We wandered toward our section leader, Molly McClelland, who was also one of the drum majors. Since we were first, she directed us to warm up in the practice room away from everyone else (being the quiet little flutes we are). After a little while, Kayla Kroder herded the flutes to the band room, and we waited patiently outside the back room to audition. By vote, they made me audition first.

The flutes finished, and then the clarinets, and so

on. When each section finished, they picked a spot in a classroom or hallway to practice and read through the music.

Inside the choir room, we took out our music, joined by the clarinets for a group sectional. Eventually Kayla wandered in, so we had all three drum majors in our room (but no saxophones- Shane and Addison were in charge of their section).

By this time it was close to 10:30 and the brass-players were still auditioning. We played through the first movement (the opener) several times, and decided to sit and chat. After all, few of us knew the freshmen well, and many of them didn't know the older crowd. Besides, this year Padawan emphasized the importance of bonding in the sections, something that could definitely be improved from the past.

Kayla, Molly, and Staci sat sprawled on the floor in a semicircle facing our arch of woodwinds. They were quietly discussing what they were to do while we talked among ourselves.

Our head drum major, Kayla Kroder, had an unusually interesting story. It was both shocking and inspiring, not to mention laced with her own brand of sarcasm.

Affectionately called "Kyle," Kayla told us her story. One of the reasons she was so excited to be drum major and lives life as much as she can was due to her family history. She was tough, and it was no surprise; her mother had passed away when she was young, much like other relatives, due to a hereditary cancer that takes victims at a young age. It was hard to believe it, but she embraced what she believed would happen when she was older and joked that she was either going to be a cop or a body guard in a big city and would "go" doing something useful, *only after* she would get to drive a neon orange lamborghini.

She was the loud drum major, particularly because it was her job. She herded us outside to John in the morning, and she was going to be the drum major who kept primary time in the show. Every inch of her was full of attitude, and she had an abrupt joking-to-serious switch at times. Even someone with freckles, brown curly hair, and blue eyes can be intimidating.

Molly was a different story. Molly was sometimes (not always!) soft spoken, normally followed instructions to the mark, and only raised her voice when she was angry or getting our attention. She was a bit more sentimental than the others (don't mention that it was her final year of marching band!) and was pretty quiet. She had straight brown hair and was shorter than most of the band members, but she took charge effectively when needed. She was also the flute section leader.

Staci, the clarinet section leader and other drum major in the trio, had short blonde hair cut to her jaw and a lot of attitude. She was no-nonsense, but liked to joke around with the collective section of flutes and clarinets when we had a free moment. Staci was the motivator, joined by Molly, and together they made us work and work until we got things right, particularly the music, which few of us had touched until auditions.

It was certainly weird being new to marching band as a *junior*. The freshmen knew each other, the sophomores seemed okay, and the only other junior in the room was Staci. I was stuck in a group where the upperclassmen were dominant and much was expected, and little was expected of freshmen- at first. So I was, without anyone coming out to say it, expected to keep up with my class and perform better faster than the young freshmen.

At about 11:20, the drum majors wrapped up their stories, and we regrouped with the rest of the band in the band room. Once more we sat (this time by section) in a circle. Mr. Padawan re-entered the room, and we eagerly awaited our placement results.

His expression wasn't as happy as we had hoped; in fact, it was a disappointed look. *Disappointed in us? Already?*

"Dudes… We've got problems. We have *holes*. On the list, we should be full on flutes, trumpets, saxophones, and tubas, and have an extra baritone, clarinet, and mellophone. Between sign-up and today… people have slipped through the cracks. *We can't let this happen.*"

He read off a list which sections had holes. There were two flute holes out of six, two trumpet holes, one clarinet space, a full saxophone section, *just* enough mellos, and still an extra baritone. That was it. There was only one extra member in the group, and a significant number of gaps in the ensemble.

When I mention holes, or gaps, it is in reference to the number of performers written into the drill, our coordinated "map" of the formations our dots create on the field. If we have a drill written expecting eight trumpets and we only have five march in the show, it will ruin the effect of some formations. Even in a basic line, it's totally noticeable when someone is missing.

During the past two years, people had quit halfway through the season or gotten injured; we had awful holes in the most important formations of last year's show, *Rhythms of a City*, which featured the St. Louis

Arch and other attractions in St. Louis, Missouri.

Those who didn't show up- if they showed up at all- would be placed last. This means they would get bottom part if the music was divided, where the top players would play a more difficult part and the ones behind them play something less difficult.

I became F3, F for flute and three for the third flute (I actually got first, but Mr. Padawan decided whether I got one or three based on the formations, since we were missing a third of our section. Several other sections did the same).

Out of all the members in marching band, one member was an extra in a section. Brian Munoz, a freshman in the competitive baritone section, was designated an alternate. Instead of marching baritone in a flute spot, he was to be a "fake," simply holding a flute for appearance and filling the hole. He was a pretty lively kid and very enthusiastic about marching.

I noticed the younger members mingling with the older students. Already groups were forming around the room. It was a tradition at Collinsville for older kids (especially in band) to pick a freshman to claim as a pal for a role of support, leadership, or even protection. It was more fun to pick several, as was evident by the numerous small groups in the band room.

Auditions and our motivational talks finally ended. *Lunchtime!*

We gorged ourselves on homemade macaroni and cheese. Afterward, we waited out the remainder of the hour and a half allotted for lunch. The afternoon's impending workout would change the tune of our feelings about marching band.

After applying sunscreen, we picked up our water

jugs and dot books and headed outside for something Padawan called *circle drill.*

We followed John to the lumpy practice field. He stopped in the middle of the right half and directed us to form a circle around him- trumpets and tubas on the yard line, mellophones and clarinets at the hash.

Many adjustments and several inspections later, we finally had an acceptable circle. The drum majors walked between us, inspecting our water jugs and black towels like circling vultures. We stood patiently under the blazing sun, squinting, wondering what we would do next. Eventually Jon took his place in the center and instructed us to set our towels in front of us, waters next, and finally music. The circle was set.

Like some of the other guys (and a few girls) in the band, John had been a part of the P90X craze. Since he was in charge of our warm-up stretches, we quickly learned those from the P90X tapes.

We stretched and bent, twisting and flexing until Padawan came outside to join us. The sun became blocked for a short period by a sheet of clouds, blanketing the sky and cooling temporarily the harsh stare of the sun that reflected off our metal instruments and into our faces.

"Pick up your horns. Hey- a little cloud love!"

There were giggles and a few enthusiastic claps.

Thus began the circle drill.

For the next hour and twenty-five minutes, we played variations of lip-slurs (and harmony), which are different scales and notes played in specific orders, and practiced step-outs. Step-outs consist of stepping out on the downbeat of the musical (or visual) exercise, taking a step back, and marking time (marching in place) for the duration of the exercise, finishing with a command "place, close." We repeated various exercises over and over to create good habits. Reviewing the fundamentals of parade band is essential for taking marching to the next level. It's a good idea to master the forward/backward marching technique before trying to march sideways.

After circle drill, it was time for fruit break.

The brief break passed, and we were sent upstairs to break down the music as a group so we could put the music on the move the next evening. *Tomorrow!* I was terrified. The idea seemed bewildering. *How on earth will we remember where we go on the field?*

It was upstairs in the band room where we discovered how difficult the music for our show really was- harder rhythms, faster tempo, and deadly intonation.

We set a circle in the band room once more, but this time we had music stands. We slowly pushed through the music that many of us had neglected, halting progress often to iron out sectional difficulties and rep (rehearsing, repetitions for reinforcement) the fixed measures.

Solaris, our show, had heavy woodwind features and difficult brass details. The lack of practice didn't make the chances of winning seem any greater, for sure- and we had only looked at the six-set opener. Each movement in *Solaris* was progressively harder than the previous, and to play harder music later in the show required stamina (which is one of the reasons we focused a great deal on tone quality and endurance with louder volumes). *Stamina? Yikes.* Half of us had tired arms (except a few woodwinds) after half an hour of playing in spot.

One member in particular had a difficult time preparing for the season- another freshman, a bari-sax-player named Maryn Kester.

Maryn Kester was five feet, eight inches tall and very slender. She was also our baritone saxophone marcher. To play the bari-sax on the move, she had to buy a special back harness and lift weights several months prior to band camp. It's truly a struggle for someone so tall and thin to hold such a large instrument; although Maryn said, "It'll be a challenge, but I'm up for it. It's marching band. It's gonna be tough."

Equally difficult instruments to hold are baritones (or in some cases, the euphonium) and tubas, but each member has their struggles.

I couldn't complain, being a flute player, but it was definitely a disadvantage, both in breathing and volume. Four flutes were just not enough.

Everyone was a little restless by the end of the music block, and some of us even slept during the hour and a half dinner break, for which we provided our own food, packed or drive-thru. Taco Bell made quite a profit off of the band kids those evenings, despite Padawan's suggestions that we avoid fast food.

The clock timed out on dinner. At last, we would set our very first formation.

Armed only with our dot books, the dot sheets with our coordinates, and four suspicious poker chips (red, blue, green and white) that we were instructed to grab, we wandered through the practice field, counting and re-marking steps, looking for our first dots. I had to ask a sophomore for help finding my dot. We stood in our spots patiently as Padawan cranked the lift into the air high above us.

"Testing one…two…three…Good. Can everyone hear me?"

We mumbled our replies. He gave the signal and a tech cranked the volume to near-deafening.

"Now?" *SCREEEEEEEEEEEEEEEE!* The microphone's whine nearly shattered our eardrums. One more adjustment, and the feedback stopped.

Several "techs" hovered nearby, adjusting rows and placing lost freshmen. Two of the past year's graduates, twin brothers Tyler and Simon Young, were busy giving directions and referring to mysterious black binders that contained charts of the formations of the drill. Techs were Padawan's experienced helpers on the field who caught mistakes as we marched or played on the field. All techs were asked back after graduating by invite-only from Mr. Padawan.

The twins- identical, in fact, who confused me for a long time- played alto saxophone and trumpet. The only easy way to tell them apart was that one smiled most of the time and wore his glasses less often than his brother. Don't ask me who was who; honestly, I *still* don't know most of the time.

Older alumni joined us too, like David Bell and a brass player for Carolina Crown named Tyler. With all the help on the ground, Mr. Padawan could focus less on small errors and more on the big picture.

"Okay. When I call your dot, raise your hand. C1, C2, T5, B2…" Padawan rolled off the numbers, and when everyone had been checked, "Drop your red poker chip between your feet."

Thus, the first dot was officially set.

Keeping the old dot in mind, we found our next three dots, placing the chips down in order. Then we moved and stood back at the very first dot.

For the first time of the season, the drum majors stepped up to the podium. Molly and Staci flanked Kayla on the smaller podiums near the thirty-five yard lines; Kayla had the tallest podium on the fifty.

We all fixed our eyes upon Kayla as she stood before the podium; then, she reached out and gripped the hand rails, pushing off the ground and ascending the steep metal stairs one at a time. At the top, she straightened, gazing out across the spattering of her peers across the bumpy field. Squinting against the sun, she gave the signal for the tech behind the ensemble to start the met (metronome); raising her hands, she gave the first downbeat of the first move of the season.

After several reps and gradually increasing the tempo, the time for rehearsal ran out. Padawan dismissed us and we left quickly.

Hot and tiring though deceptively easy, the first day of band camp 2011 wrapped up neatly and quietly as we drove into the sunset to our homes for the night.

Later Kayla recalled, "I was absolutely terrified. I mean, in marching band you have an idea of what the drum major should be, and I was really scared to mess up in front of everyone. After all, if I mess up, the whole thing could fall apart."

Like Atlas in mythology holding the world on his shoulders for all eternity, Kayla held the weight of the marching band on her shoulders, as did Staci and Molly, and they were certainly taking that task seriously.

The question was, were *we* ready to take our jobs seriously?

Chapter 2: Trial by Fire

Band Camp Day 2- July 26, 2011

It was hotter than blazes, and the sun was only halfway risen.

Smelling of sunscreen, a pack of band students marched into the band room to gather their towels, dot books, hats, and sunglasses. There was still enthusiasm, but it was duller than the previous day. The heat and Padawan's promise of rigorous basics and drill outside until lunch did little to boost our confidence.

Suspiciously, the veterans of marching band were all a little too quiet.

Promptly at 8:55, John Bailey began kicking people out of the band room. "Come on guys; we're about to *start.*" His good-natured but firm nagging encouraged most of us to hurry outside. The less obedient members lazily strolled outside, testing the patience of section leaders and the leadership team alike. Padawan was still inside his office.

Oncc morc placing our towels and waters in rows on the sideline, we formed a parade block. John and Kayla put us into rows, spacing us exactly two steps apart in the row and four steps between each row. After the arrangement was approved, we were allowed to put our instruments down on our towels in a uniform manner in front of us. John led us through warm up stretches; the hot, sweaty morning routine had begun.

Tuesday- the second day- was arguably the worst morning of the whole band camp. We were disillusioned by the time spent the previous morning lounging on the floor practicing scales and staring at our music and the cloudy, cool afternoon rehearsals. There would be no more mornings hanging around inside for the rest of the camp, and there would be very few rehearsals held inside because of the weather.

As we bent over to touch our toes and stretch our muscles, the sun glared arrogantly on our cotton-clad backs. There wasn't the slightest bit of breeze or trace of a cloud in the sky, which was intensely blue and difficult to look at without squinting. Every student wore shorts or capris and ankle socks, and most brought sunglasses or a brimmed hat. Personally, I'd always hated baseball caps, but now I genuinely appreciate them. I had an easier time keeping cool and avoiding facial sunburns because of my trusty red hat.

Our bodies were already glistening with a coat of sweat when Padawan emerged from the plain square building containing the band room and the cafeteria.

It looked like we would be having a long morning.

Last night, when chattering excitedly at the table with my family about the day's experiences, my brother was very quiet. He quickly ate his snack, chugged his glass of milk, and answered only simple questions when asked. The only thing he said was, "Just wait until tomorrow."

"It can't be that difficult. Today was easy."

"Just wait."

Here we were under the sun and he was right. I was terribly, awfully wrong. I had expected just a longer time outside. Maybe the morning wouldn't have been so bad if we weren't in the middle of a "St. Louis Summer" and the temperature with the heat index wasn't *one hundred and three degrees*! The humidity was cranked to eighty percent; we were practically *inhaling* clouds. Every moment seemed to increase the intensity of the heat beating upon us and made us feel as though we were being cooked alive, roasted like a hundred Thanksgiving turkeys. The St. Louis Metro area is known for its extremely hot and humid summers; luckily, many water breaks throughout the morning sustained us.

For a little while, I actually thought that I would sweat to death.

The hour and a half long morning "basics block" kicked our butts and shifted our bodies into high gear. Basics are a lot harder than they appear. It takes focus and muscle control in the legs and ankles and a good technique to survive. Coming off of a long and lazy summer break, many of us were ill-prepared for the exertion. The burning in our calves and thighs hinted at the future muscles we would enjoy later in the season.

For this morning, the basics were fairly simple. The first techniques we reviewed briefly involved step-outs backwards and forwards. Following that was something we call factory.

Factory is a parade block exercise. We were lined up with seven members across, two measured steps apart and four steps between rows. The first line marches forward for eight counts, holds eight counts, and marches again. The next row then steps off with the first. (Every sixteen counts the next row marches… like a factory). The goal is to keep lines even and reach the desired five yards exactly, with the correct foot, on the right count, and preferably together as a row. The exercise begins facing forward and at a moderate tempo (the speed, or beats per minute), but gradually switches to backward and side marching and varying tempos. Essentially, it mimics a production line's uniformity. We focused only on forward and backward during this rehearsal, but Padawan assured us ominously that we would soon practice factory side-to-side.

The routine itself was not very difficult at moderate tempos, but our traditional straight-leg marching technique made it much more difficult and builds more muscle in the legs. Our "roll-steps" are how we step smoothly without jarring and breaking our sounds while moving and playing, and make the visually-appealing marching style possible.

Factory finished as the sun climbed slowly toward the highest point in the sky, still a cloudless blue dome above us. The birds that did fly above us were few and far in between. Most living creatures had the sense to stay in the shade on a day like this.

Not us. We would dutifully overcome the heat as Padawan directed. As each moment ticked by on the clock, we dripped sweat in silence and followed directions as given. The time passed excruciatingly slow for those of us who weren't very athletic or experienced. The morning's newspaper reported high temperatures that scared other bands off their practice fields and advised strongly against strenuous outdoor activities.

Not us.

In years past, Collinsville had often been referred to as "the little guys." We've suffered because of our poor size ratio to that of our general student body of two thousand at competitions like the Ozarko competition, which was judged based on school size. We competed last year with an ensemble of roughly seventy-six members against giant bands with nearly two hundred. Even playing at our loudest volume, our fate was usually sealed; size really does matter in marching band.

Small bands receive a different kind of advantage

on the field. When you know every single face around you and can tell which members are nearby in the formations, it's somewhat easier to learn how to move together on the field and function as one body. With everyone connected, we could learn each other's strengths and weaknesses to adjust better on the field. The fluid teamwork that we needed to form would make or break the season.

It seemed a bit early to us to think about teamwork. The general attitude was, "Why now? I'm trying to learn my stuff, you're trying to learn yours; you do your thing and I'll do mine." (And the color guard had yet to rehearse with us outside, as we hadn't yet put any of the music on the move.) The accuracy of each dot was stressed more than the formation- for the moment. It was too early to learn our dots otherwise.

Mr. Padawan checked his watch; satisfied with progress, he allowed an extra water break in the shade.

It was hot even in the shade. The backs of our throats burned with an unquenchable thirst for water. (Being the English nerd that I am, I even cracked a joke that I loved my water so much, I was considering writing a sonnet about it.) And how hard it was to pace ourselves! It was *so* tempting to chug water, until we reconsidered the heat and what it might do to our stomachs while marching. The section leaders around us watched their sections like hawks; the flutes and clarinets felt very alone on the field.

"Ok. Run on back to your spots." Most groaned and stumbled back dragging their feet. A few trumpets and baritones actually ran. Mr. Padawan noted their hustle briefly.

The parade block was formed once more facing the school's vocational area. Small bees hovered near our ankles, making some of the woodwinds nervous as we waited for Padawan's instructions.

Mr. Padawan was not on the lift for any of the "basic" exercises. He walked or stood near us the whole time, making corrections and offering information as necessary; being on the lift (the "eye in the sky") impractical for demonstrating marching techniques. He was not the tallest guy who ever marched, but not the shortest, either. He was dressed like us in athletic shorts and a T-shirt, a complete change from his "band director" outfit he wore every single day at school: formal pants and a drum corps polo. It was still weird seeing him dressed that way and wearing tennis shoes instead of dress shoes, but he was all about being a team. He was not marching a show- we were. He was not the one marching in circles or five by five- we were. He *could* have stood to the side and wear a suit while we sweat and let techs demonstrate the techniques. Instead, teamwork prevailed. Plus, it would be odd for a drum corps leader to opt out of marching and sweating while instructing a marching band.

That fact passed unnoticed by many of the students griping about the heat and the exercises. Grasshoppers chirped angrily as they flew away from our crushing feet while we marched or shuffled around in the dusty blades of grass. The patchy grass that still existed in our lumpy field wouldn't last long, Padawan had assured us, and then we would inhale the dust we kicked up, which would coat our throats and instruments by October. The dust that was already painting our ankles brown and sticking to our sweat did little to help the charring effects of the sun and the hot, still air.

Padawan waited for all pairs of eyes to turn towards him.

"Ready to do something hard?"

Our silence answered for us.

Padawan clapped his hands together. "Okay, Band. You're receiving information. Pay attention." He moved directly in front of the first row and stood with his back to us. Turning to talk over his shoulder, he shifted to "standby" mode, holding an invisible horn at *carry position* (not out and up in front to play, but more comfortably bell-down with bent elbows in front of his chest). "You're going to learn how to change directions. Watch my feet. To step out *left*," he said, shifting his feet, "this is easy, take your first step with your left foot at an angle to your left." He demonstrated as we craned our necks to see around other members. "Now you try."

As each moment of concentration passed and we absorbed the techniques like little sponges, in all that sweat and heat, there was unmistakable pride and effort. Maybe half of the pride stemmed from Mr. Padawan's pep-talks and the fact that we were one of the few bands practicing in this heat. It seemed that every few minutes Mr. Padawan complemented us on something and immediately pushed us harder.

"Let's go to the right now. This one is tricky. Go to standby, bring your left foot across your right, aiming toward your right side- yes, I know this isn't comfortable- and place it heel down, toe up. Right! Try it."

We wobbled unsteadily as we followed his instructions. Nobody fell.

"Excellent! Time for our next exercise."

He moved us very quickly through the exercises. It worried me. I was already feeling overwhelmed and struggling to keep up in the heat.

Though time grew short as we soared through basics before setting our next dots, we managed to learn how to "slide" backward right and left. As complicated as it seems, it was actually as simple as pointing the right toe (the command called "place" in marching terms) away from the direction desired; literally, just doing a forward slide, *backwards*.

That was "basics." Several freshman and newbie (a.k.a., me and Rachel) heads were starting to spin.

After a slightly extended water break, it was back to the poker chips and dot sheets for us. The poker chips quickly became sweaty and sticky in our palms while Mr. Padawan organized the techs and re-checked the mic.

The first movement of our show, *Solaris*, had only six dots. The first seventy-six counts of the show were filled solely with the percussion. At letter D the woodwinds enter, signaling the first step out of the show. Dots one through four were set the day before in the afternoon, leaving only two to finish setting the intro. From there on our task would be to rep the section until it runs smoothly and begin setting the dots for the second movement. There was no separation between the first movement (the intro) and the second.

It sounded easy enough…right?

Dot five, we learned shortly, would be a hold in the music. The color guard would have a flag feature while we stood in place with our horns aimed at the "box," bells tilted twenty-five degrees higher than the normal playing position. The "Box" is the general area at the height were the judges sit at our final competition of the season, The Greater St. Louis Marching Band Festival, GSL for short.

From the first day of the season, this was everything. This was what we worked for the whole season: placement at GSL.

Dot five marked the beginning of a long struggle with…forming a straight line. It was supposed to be easy, yet someone near the center was slightly off and skewed the line. We could not look away from Kayla, so we relied almost completely on peripheral vision.

I wasn't the only one concerned about our ability to line up. Mr. Padawan called us out, forewarning that circles would be much more difficult. *Solaris* was about the sun; we would see a whole bunch of circles throughout the show and practice them until we were setting them in our sleep.

Yikes.

"Okay. Drop your first chip between your feet. Go find your next dot."

Our shuffling feet carelessly scattered the low-flying bees. Tiny ant hills dotted the dirt patches. We eyed these tiny land mines warily as we stood waiting once more for instructions.

The rest of the time block for dots went without problems, except for some chips getting kicked around and lost while marching. We managed to set dots nine and ten before lunch break. Mr. Padawan and the techs seemed pleased with our progress, although it seemed we had barely accomplished anything.

Before releasing us, Mr. P. told us a story. He always talks about his friends who also direct bands that live out east. At the beginning of summer he announced to them that we were to play *Solaris*. *Solaris* was known for its high level of difficulty, both musically and the expectations for visual performance of it (circles, since it was the sun). Padawan looked directly at us and said,

"When they heard, they laughed." So did the directors of our neighboring schools. "You're playing *that*?"

"This year, we've got something to prove. We're the little guys, and we're taking on Goliath. We have *never* won our class at GSL. But it can't be done unless you work hard. This show is going to push you. It's not an easy show. With it, if we can do this...we have a shot at winning."

It was just a little something to chew on over lunch break.

Lunch was the best thing all day for me. The morning was my punishment for limiting strenuous exercise to gym class and goofing off at home. The humidity and the roasting sunlight made me feel like I was just going to fall over and burn to a crisp. St. Louis summers can be harsh to those accustomed to staying indoors. All morning I wished I was in my nice, cool room in bed instead of outside in the heat. If only...

I was secretly glad that I had worn shorts, even as self-conscious of my legs as I am. (Eventually I learned that people don't judge in marching band, and that it was okay to walk around in pink *happy bunny* shorts with long black socks before and after performances.) If I had even tried wearing anything longer, I would have dropped in the heat on the field.

To top everything off, I felt so awkward and uncoordinated. A few times I stepped off on the wrong foot, and other times I missed my dot by a large margin. It seemed like I was the *only one* panicking on the field when we had to find our dots without the poker chips.

I began to seriously doubt that marching band would be a good experience for me. I was so frustrated that I was falling behind so quickly, that I wouldn't be able to survive all the exercise and the heat; worst of all, Zach would never let me forget it. Padawan would be upset, my parents would be angry, and my friends would all be disappointed in me. I couldn't see any alternative to quitting, though. The group would be better off without me because I was confused and had overestimated what I could do. I felt that I had made a *huge* mistake joining marching band.

These feelings didn't digest as well as my lunch did. Failure doesn't sit well with me.

After lunch, the different sections met briefly for sectionals, reapplied sunscreen, and headed out for circle drill.

We finally got a taste of the real circle drill. Circle drill was a critical warm up before all competitions and performances; we even used it before parades.

It also happened to involve forming a circle.

The sun was a bit less intense after lunch than it was in the morning. At 1:30, it was higher in the sky, and the humidity had finally dropped from the smothering eighty percent.

I shuffled outside, one of the less enthusiastic of the pack. We were moving very fast, and my whole lunch hour had been tainted dreading the rest of the season. It doesn't take much stress or imagination to inspire horrible daydreams about totally freezing on the field in performance, a fear most freshmen surrounding me had mentioned. The season stretched ahead like a marathon and I was the one hobbling behind, trying to keep up desperately. I was *sure* I would be the embarrassment of the group.

Zach was right. There was no way I would last the season, not even the two weeks of band camp.

Like our first day, as we set the circle we were rearranged until it no longer looked so lumpy. The techs wove between us and corrected the "corners" that appeared when people moved around to talk to their friends.

There wasn't a cloud in the sky above. I was glad I had my clip-on shades for my glasses. The sky was still too bright to look at directly.

Mr. Padawan strolled from the building to the center of the circle holding a pair of wooden drumsticks and his green water cooler. He looked pleased.

He looked around before addressing us, assessing our expressions.

"Welcome back. We've all had lunch and a nice break, the humidity's gone down, and there's a bit of a breeze. This morning went great; you guys were *excellent*! It is so awesome, the way you guys come out here and practice." He paused, smiling and shaking his head, and looked directly at us, turning to talk to everyone. "Dudes- if you keep up the effort you've shown today… we could be *unstoppable.* We could *win* this."

The whole time I was lost. Doing well? Yes, everyone else was, but not me.

I pondered these compliments for the rest of the day. I was surviving the heat much better then, not nearly as dizzy and not as wobbly as earlier. It had cooled slightly over lunch, and *everyone* appreciated the change.

"Okay. Ready? Pick up your instruments." He paused for us to pick up our instruments and turn our eyes back towards him. The light glinted in every direction from the many metal horns lying on black towels. "Go to standby."

One of the most important problems we needed to tackle would be air support and volume. In drum corps, the extreme shows and hard core practices require good breathing, as do high school bands in theirs. *Solaris* was about ten minutes long. To sustain the higher notes and build up our endurance for its quick tempos, we would need a strong technique.

Techniques, techniques; where would we be without them?

The most "breathing" experience the majority of us have had in the last year was playing our instruments while sitting in chairs. On our feet and moving we would need steady support and supply. Padawan, like always, had it all planned.

"The first thing we do, and *should* do before playing, is our breathing exercise. The way you breathe and approach the horn will affect your attack. In this exercise, you will step out after eight clicks," (he used his drumsticks to amplify the beats), "air-only, and practice attacking the note in time with the met." (Met is band slang for metronome.)

"Horns up!"

When his hands came up, our horns snapped from carry to playing position. All eyes were locked on him as he whipped out the drumsticks. "One, two, one, two, three, *breathe…*" we all thought; and, focusing on the steady tempo, stepped out to the wheeze of air rattling through our dusty horns.

"Okay… Not bad. Let's try that again."

After a succession of attempts, we produced a louder, more satisfying hiss.

"That was better. Your attacks were stronger, you used more air, and they were in time. We'll work on this more as the season progresses. For now, we'll try step-outs to lip slurs, keeping attack and air support in mind."

The afternoon's circle drill became a standard for warm-up, the basic routine. We played the lip slurs once more; only, with a twist we hadn't expected.

The first time rehearsing the new technique, we used chromatic long tones. Using the chromatic scale, we took eight steps backward (switching the note after each eight counts), eight forward (back to circle), eight more backward, and then froze while Mr. Padawan taught us the challenging part of circle drill. We switched our hips so that we were facing forward to march to our right around the circle. To our right, we marched eight, started back up the chromatic scale on the next eight, and then pointed our toes to reverse. We returned with two sets of eight back around, and then sustained concert F as we marched the eight final counts forward back to our original spots in the circle.

Phew! I thought this was a lot more confusing than remembering where the first ten dots of the show were.

Learning that and several other variations took the rest of the circle drill block. We headed back inside for fruit break and then musical block, hopefully to put the opener (the first movement, which was the first six dots of our show) on the move musically after dinner.

The musical block picked up exactly where the last one left off. Again, we set a squished circle around the band room as the section leaders set up stands.

Those of us who weren't playing sat cross-legged while Padawan worked with each section. Some picked at the carpet, while some whispered among their sections. After the morning's workout, many of us longed for the summer we had started, lazy and air-conditioned. At least the majority of us didn't have any sunburns yet.

The clarinets sitting nearby dutifully fingered through their parts while they were waiting. All of the reeds and flutes had noticed a difficult woodwind feature lurking close in the music. At letter O, in measures of 5/4 time signature, there was a large splotch of black notes swimming ominously across the page. They were high, with odd rests squeezed between. It wouldn't be so hard at the average march tempo of one hundred and twenty beats per minute… except this part of the piece was marked for one hundred and sixty-four.

Not too much of the second movement was difficult. The first was all ready to put on the field later. It was just that part, letter O. I could only imagine us trying to change directions while playing it. Maybe we would only have to go straight, or we would have a hold there…

The more I thought about it, the more I considered quitting the whole thing. It seemed like I would and could quit, except I had placed first in auditions on flute part, only second to Molly. That made me feel like *I* was the one who had to set a good example and had to stick it out no matter what happened to me. Quitting on the second day of band camp would bring truth to Padawan's speech about people dropping out and ruin the chances of avoiding holes in the program this year… after all, about sixty-five members wasn't much to work with for formations. Losing another member means another hole to fill, and another injury to the program.

I gave up thinking about it and endured the rest of musical block.

Dinner came and went quickly after the long rehearsal. I had foolishly brought nothing to do after I had eaten my dinner, so I just sat there up in the band hallway. Many of the others knew their peers well; I am a bit more shy, so I generally kept to myself.

Quickly I realized this was impossible in band. *Everyone* was connected. Friends would be made when so much time was spent together; it was as simple as that.

One of the two female baritone-players walked over to sit by me. Melissa was my age, short with long brown hair and rosy cheeks. She was one of my friends from other classes and wanted to chat.

The other new marching flautist, Rachel, joined us as well. She didn't have a whole crowd her age experiencing marching band for the first time to talk with like the freshmen did, either, and was also shy. My spot near one of the windows in the hallway was starting to get crowded; that was okay with me.

More wandered over out of boredom throughout the break and quite innocently a new group of friends formed: long-legged Maryn, the bari-sax player; cute little Andrew with freckles, a baritone-player; Mat the trumpet-player; and many more.

It wasn't much later when Mat admitted, "When we started learning the basics, I was overwhelmed; in a word, 'CRAP!' I was about ready to quit, but what changed my mind was that I was making friends who would have my back."

Band students who didn't bring their dinner

carpooled in loud groups to the nearby McDonald's or played with a tennis ball in the spacious band room. Freshmen were with seniors, guard with band and pit- even sectional rivals hung out together. The atmosphere had its own magnetic pull. If it were not for the actual rehearsals, it would look like someone had magically gotten cheerleaders, athletes, math teamers, and English nerds together to have a blast, and nobody would be able to repeat the experiment. The secret ingredient X was music. The band was a family, and everyone was accepted if they accepted others.

Dinner ended. Peanut butter sandwiches with extra strawberry jelly squishing out the sides are always very comforting.

It was time to hit the field.

Patiently we stood waiting for Kayla, Molly, and Staci to climb on top of their heavy metal podiums.

Setup for the last field rehearsal of the day was carricd out by some of the band students over their break, with their own manpower. Everyone sat on the floor lazily for the last twenty minutes of break or ran around laughing while Kayla, Staci and Molly dragged their podiums into the elevator and outside. Jordan and John had to fetch the lift from the other side of the school and drive it over to the field at walking speed. My brother volunteered to carry the sound cart outside for each rehearsal, down the stairs and out to the back sideline, where he then checked the battery and tested equipment. They all had extra responsibilities that took extra time and effort to ensure that rehearsal ran smoothly.

When Kayla reached the top, she looked over our

heads, raised her hands, and signaled the tech running the metronome to begin. Molly and Staci mirrored every beat.

The first repetition was air-only while holding our instruments to remember our dots. The more experienced marchers sought out their dots with more confidence than the beginners, but the beginners made just as much effort. We were all striving to please, to reach out and make a mark this year. We were tired of *losing*. Each rehearsal to us was one more step toward a competition, not one less day we had to work hard. We had barely begun, and our eyes were set on the prize.

"Reset! We'll go D to E, twenty-four counts; *everyone's in*."

We hustled back to our first dots. A few people cheered and whooped.

"First musical rep on the move of the season." Padawan clicked off the mic.

Kayla cleared her throat from atop the podium and repeated the instructions. She nodded at the tech running the metronome.

Thud, thud, thud, thud.

The saxophones began with a lively dancing melody that the flutes and clarinets echoed. The brass attacked their first note.

Kayla cut off the note with a wave of her hands.

The rehearsal and the day alike ended on a high note at letter G. As the sun slowly crawled down from its peak in the sky, we dragged our weary feet off the field and towards the parking lot. Sustaining our enthusiasm was just as draining as the physical exercises, if not more. Excitement is an adrenaline rush with the notable energy crash afterward.

The second day of band camp came to a close. I

left silently, lost in thought in the windy back seat of Dominick's truck until we reached my house. I was the tag-along; Zach was his second in command and one of his good buddies. I was just one wandering flute player in the middle of the marching band.

All night I tossed and turned, wrestling with the inevitable in my mind: my parents were paying for me to do this, and I would be letting them- and all my friends- down if I quit.

There was nothing I could really do. Nothing would change.

This is going to be a long season...

Chapter 3: "Green Lantern!"

Band Camp Day 3- July 27, 2011

The moment the sun peeked between the blinds in my room, I groaned and rolled over, trying to fall back asleep. It was useless. My alarm clock could easily be ignored, but not Zach's constant banging on my bedroom door and the glaring bright light invading my sleeping zone. I eventually gave in and crawled out of bed. After throwing on my marching clothes and choking down an "everything" bagel covered in poppy seeds, I ran out the door after Zach to catch my ride to band camp.

The sunny bright skies promised a day like those we had already survived: not quite as humid, but potentially as difficult to endure. "The worst rehearsal was over," the veterans told me, "You'll get used to the heat." I recognized one thing rather quickly: the heavier cotton T-shirts I had worn the previous days had increased how hot it seemed while marching. The tank top I had thrown on in the morning allowed my skin to breathe- I was already a lot cooler than on the other days! Others had gotten the same idea, I noticed.

Perhaps this won't be too bad. It's about survival, after all. I can do that. Even the freshmen are surviving! Maybe I can do this...

For the first time during band camp, a few little fluffy clouds rolled across the sky overhead. None managed to stay long or black out the sun for more than a minute, but their presence was a relief anyway.

"G-O-O-D M-O-R-N-I-N-G! GOOD MORNING, BAND! GOOD MORNING!" Our enthusiastic drum majors attempted to pump up the excitement in the morning with a loud wake up cheer. That morning it worked.

Basics flew away with the clouds and the little moths that fluttered across the field. We practiced factory again, improving from the previous day as much as possible. Mr. Padawan commented that our postures didn't resemble those of couch potatoes this morning. Progress was definitely under way.

The cooler morning (the heat index said it was in the mid-nineties!) and the focus on our marching techniques in factory began to repair my fractured confidence and also of others around me. I saw more smiles on faces than grim expressions, and heard fewer complaints.

We had more practice getting the feel of our step sizes from yard line to yard line and becoming more aware of our front-to-back locations on the field. If nothing else went well for the day, at least the confidence in our strides would take us someplace.

Oh water jug; how much I do love thee in the heat....

After a brief moment of wandering, we were instructed to find the last dot we had set, dot ten. On one side of the field, the woodwinds were making little triangle formations while the brass and saxes were forming their circles. The section leaders had already passed out the new dot sheets for movement two. Most of us had ours written in our dot books; those of us who neglected to were subjected to Padawan's lecture about losing dot sheets and being responsible.

"Go find the dot before this one, dot nine." We grumbled and groaned quietly as we shuffled around. The bumpy grass pits and dirt mounds made walking around a nuisance. Brian, the "extra" freshman assigned to march flute for the season, hopped around impatiently behind me.

One of the marching techs was rearranging and straightening the woodwind forms; he moved on from the clarinets and flipped a page in his black binder as he approached our wedge. "F3- move to your right-okay, stop. F6- back up."

It was one big waiting game. Every dot still needed checked and adjusted before moving on, especially from one day to the next. At least the few moments of stillness gave us time to clear our thoughts.

"Alright. Taking it from dot nine, we'll move eight counts to dot ten at one hundred and thirty-two beats per minute." Several of the brass members were less patient and were talking. Being such close friends in a sport with long hours, it was *so* irresistible…

"Hey! Guys! Kayla has your attention now, you're about to move. There's no need to be talking. Okay, go, Kayla." Mr. Padawan clicked off the mic and watched us from the lift.

The lift was a small cherry-picker that drove very slowly and cranked up about thirty feet above the ground for a bird's eye view of the formations. The bleachers could function as well as the lift to some extent if we were eventually allowed to use the football field. Either way, the height advantage would help Mr. Padawan spot the dots that need adjustments.

Beneath the "eye in the sky" (another nickname for the lift), we had our own atmosphere of concentration. It was written on our faces and even laced into our shoes as we cut our paths through the tired grass on the field. If there were any members who were not completely engrossed with their dots, they pretended exceptionally well.

Push one, two, three, four... I thought of nothing but my dot, forcing my feet to operate in time with the metronome and Kayla's hands. *Gotta get there...gotta get there...c'mon feet...* For me, the next dot involved a direction change. I finally began to get the hang of placing my foot and pushing off simultaneously without popping my ankle and wobbling.

Push forward, two, three, four... It was still roasting hot. I was thirsty, and my mouth was dry. In the muscles in my shoulders and arms, I felt a dull aching that would probably inhibit movement of my arms later. Beyond all that, beyond all the doubts and difficulties, I was finally *getting* it.

"Okay, everyone has their dots, yes? Review time is over. Time to find dot eleven." The dot was set within minutes. Atop the lift, Mr. Padawan opened his mouth to speak, stopped, and frowned at his binder. "...eleven, twelve... Did I give you guys the subsets?" *Subsets?* I studied my dot sheet, and then I could tell why. I had to go all the way from the middle of side one to the fifty. It said the move was thirty-two counts, but if I had to move in a straight line to my dot, thirty-two counts would be way too many.

It had to be harder than that. Padawan said our show would be difficult, and I expected nothing less.

Molly and Staci joined the other leaders distributing their section's dots, temporarily deserting their podiums. Mr. Padawan allowed us a few moments to set the subsets and tuck the sheets into our dot books. The two drum majors climbed back onto their podiums. Kayla had been waiting patiently the whole time, sweating in the direct light that was also reflecting off of the podium onto her skin. "Ready?" she called. "Going to subset eleven-A, eight counts...*set!*"

With the new subsets, the brass would form a circle and move in a straight line through a space where the woodwinds were currently standing. This update would funnel the woodwinds into a straight line in eight counts, across the field in that line for sixteen counts, and shooting off in different directions, finishing off in rows across the field.

I felt like I was part of a waiting game on a placemat at a restaurant. Connect the dots, make lines. Become a part of a box. Reset. Lines, move left, shoot backward. (My last dot was so far back that I was practically leaping backward to make it, a dot I would struggle with all season.) Reset. Run, reset. Run, reset.

"You can't see it now," Mr. Padawan remarked, leaning on his elbow against the lift's rail, "but this move resembles something from current pop culture. I'm sure you guys will all recognize this. Reset." He watched us prepare to step out. "Ready?" When we hit our first subset, dot eleven-A, and began to slide left as the brass circle slid right, he yelled, "GREEN LANTERN!"

I was laughing and feebly trying to keep my arms up with my dot book held to my face like a flute as we completed the move. The morning shriveled up in the sunshine that we were learning to survive in. When Padawan released us for lunch, we had set up to dot nineteen, a stretch which included holds and tiny movements that would involve "body" sections.

The woodwinds' infamous musical feature loomed

over our heads like a sword on a string, ready to fall and pin us in our places and halt progress. "Be prepared for a workout in musical block," our section leaders cautioned. "We're tackling *letter O* today. Come upstairs for lunch. Then we're going to practice." *Gulp.*

The chilled air-conditioned cafeteria revived our sweating bodies as we ate. Once more we wolfed down our food (generously served) and greatly appreciated the hard work of the parents in the school kitchen. The lights were bright, but seemed as dim as little Christmas lights. What a relief it was to sit down!

It was one of the mellophone-players' birthday. As if on cue, Dominick and some of the other upperclassmen brass players exploded into an extremely loud version of "Happy Birthday" followed by loud chants and cheers from people around him.

Zach cracked a joke that stuck. He was tired of the "ups", like wake-ups, push-ups, and sit-ups. So now he would focus on the "downs", like sit-downs, chow-downs, and lay-downs. I was ready to embrace this philosophy completely. Unfortunately, he never stuck to it.

I stopped briefly in the bandroom where I had left my sun shades. To cross the room and access my locker, I had to dodge a flying water bottle and two tennis balls from two separate groups throwing them around. Unlike the woodwinds led by Molly and Staci, *most* of the brass sections sat and talked through lunch and threw practice out the window. *You can lead a horse to water……*

The other flutes and clarinets were sitting or lying on the cool speckled floor in the chorus room. I sat down heavily next to Trevor, the only flute besides Molly who wasn't completely new to this sport.

Time was ticking. In a hurry to reapply sunscreen before starting to break down letter O, I smeared on what I could before wiping my hands on my T-shirt so I could keep my flute from sliding in my slimy grip.

Kayla deserved a *lot* of credit during the difficult lunch rehearsal. At first, letter O was brutal. It lasted eight measures in the 5/4 time signature, and it was marked to be played at *one hundred and sixty-four beats per minute.* It was all eighth and sixteenth notes! But not once did she lose her patience with us, even when our attempts were pitiful and had little result. Measure by measure she pulled us through, sometimes as if by will power alone. Both she and Molly clapped and sang out our parts for us. I could tell that they were frustrated too. What was Padawan *thinking*, giving us a show piece like this?

There were only fifteen minutes left of the sectional, and by chance, something clicked. A clarinet got it, then another, then two flutes, and moments later, the majority of us were thrusting those notes out as fast as our fingers could squeeze the keys. We fiercely dragged the stragglers to our tempo with each repetition and speed increase, forcing them to sink or swim.

Molly and Staci (who had been running a metronome) had ear-to-ear smiles as we adjourned our session and rejoined the others for circle drill. "I can't wait till Padawan hears *this* later."

Our budding excitement was suppressed for the longest time. Circles *never* end…or so it seems. Instead of learning new lip slurs or practicing marching in our circle, things were about to spin in a whole new direction: volume control.

Last year at competition, my fellow band members had performed at competitions hours and hours away, and there were even a few that included an overnight stay at a hotel. At one of those competitions, while waiting, they saw little bands playing their hearts out with fewer than ninety members and some of the colossal bands playing softly and lazily, with many members hiding behind each other. Those giant bands had an abundance of members, yet they didn't use their full potential. Our ears should have been ringing from a powerful surge of sound, but instead…nothing. Bands like that lose the true magic of a *marching band.*

If marching band was meant for soft, fluffy music and weak fanfare, then why would anyone be outside marching at all? Marching band breathes life into music, giving it a pulse, a soul that is tangible, emanating from the formations like ripples from a rock crashing into a pond. It is the inspiration of music, with its own theme and action, thundering and dancing across the field like lightning or a soft rain. The whole reason to play out and to be heard is to show power; and the players are the supercharged conductors. It was time to let the music explode from within us.

"Good afternoon, band! We've made wonderful progress this morning. We've had a nice break. Unfortunately, the clouds have left us, but it has certainly cooled down from yesterday." We nodded and whispered among ourselves at those comments. Mr. Padawan pushed his sunglasses up. "Yesterday, we set the circle and practiced marching in time with lip slurs. Hard stuff, yeah? Today is a little bit of a break- sort of. We're going to focus on field dynamics."

This was no surprise to us; everything we had

played on the field so far was currently at a stagnant volume of mezzo-forte (medium). It was all we could manage at the moment. Marching takes plenty of air, and so does playing an instrument by itself. Putting the two together sucks every ounce of air from our lungs faster than a vacuum cleaner! If we wanted to last longer than the opening of the show, we needed to listen and practice anything Mr. Padawan taught us.

"Oh! He's gonna teach us breathing gym!" said Trevor, the only guy who played flute in the band this year. During the previous year, in an odd twist, our secondary band had four flute players, three of whom were guys, and then there was me, leader the pack. Then the situation had flipped, with girls taking the majority, leaving Trevor by himself. He was sarcastic and liked to tease, but he was a dependable member of the band.

"Breathing gym?" I whispered.

"Yeah. You'll see."

"All right, first we're going to do a little *breathing gym.* Incumbent marchers, you know what this is. First: stand with your feet shoulder-width apart and relax; bend your knees a little. Great! Form an O with your right hand- like this." Padawan demonstrated, turning to show everyone. "And now make a small O with your mouth." He paused. "You guys are kind of squished together. Spread out; inside or outside the circle, doesn't matter. Just make some space."

I was distracted by an airplane flying over us, high above our little group. It was so high up, much nearer to the sun than us. The rays beamed across our passing witness, melting warmly on our faces. It was shortly out of sight, drifting silently as it disappeared.

"Is everyone ready?" Padawan asked. I had

accidentally missed the instructions while gazing at the airplane, as circle drill wasn't the most exciting exercise to rehearse. So I stood there, watching and mimicking the pose everyone else was in, waiting to find out the exercise.

Mr. Padawan raised his drum sticks and counted off. On the downbeat, everyone gulped in air for four counts and exhaled out for four counts. "Half notes. And-go." Breathe in for two counts, out for two. I jumped into the exercise. Several woodwind and brass players near me wobbled. The rapid bursts of air made me dizzy, and now I could see why Padawan made us bend our knees.

"Quarter notes. Go." Sixteen counts later, we sucked in as much air as we could in one count, raising our arms up, and sighed out, dropping our arms to our sides. We coughed and sputtered while we recovered and straightened up. Obviously, it would take a while for our individual air capacities to increase. But that was only one of the two exercises of breathing gym. For the time being, we were moving forward to dynamics.

Someone whistled the *Jeopardy!* theme as we stood in the field reforming the circle. Most of us looked a little tired, probably because of the breathing exercises. A few moments later, Padawan attended to us. He said something to Tyler, the marching tech from DCI, and turned to us. "Okay. Next, everyone will play the chord at the two measures before letter I in the second movement. It's a D-major chord. Taking it up to speed, you will attack at mezzo forte and crescendo. The actual volume written is quadruple forte, but we're not there yet. We'll practice getting louder throughout band camp and as the season progresses, but for now we'll increase in increments." He pushed up his sunglasses. "Go to standby."

We stood up straight and yawned before hoisting our horns to our mouths, taking measures to keep the circle neat. Group after group played their notes in the chord to tune. After tuning, we were then to play that chord each time Mr. Padawan gave us a down beat, and as he motioned upward with one hand, we would increase our volume by one level, and the goal was to stay in tune. When our time for circle drill had elapsed, our volume grew all the way up to fortissimo, or double forte. It would be a while before our little band could comfortably and confidently attack notes at quadruple forte volume on the move.

For our fruit break each day, we were expected to stand in a long line and move around the fruit cart with haste. Several parent volunteers stand at the cart to shovel grapes, orange wedges, apple slices, or a banana (or all) into a large Styrofoam cup for each of us. The strawberries and the grapes went the fastest, whereas there were always extras of oranges and apples. Despite the discouragement from the parents, a few people got away with throwing grapes around, and I'm not really sure they were all freshmen, either.

After our break, we all trudged upstairs to the bandroom for the "inside" circle. It was time for us woodwinds to show off our noon time accomplishments.

Mr. Padawan started the musical block by announcing that the woodwinds were going to show off for everyone and play letter O up to tempo. Our first attempt was decent; the saxophones saved us. More of the clarinets had most of it down, or at least to cover where others left off. In the flute section, well, we needed some work. About three of us had it figured out. After we worked through it a few more times, Mr. Padawan turned to the brass. It was time for them to play their parts.

Each brass section struggled through different sections, which improved greatly with several repeats, and the players relaxed only when the next section was in the hot seat. The resting sections flopped onto the floor and fingered through their parts, eager to work ahead. The more finger practice we could get in, the better. It would save us time that would be spent on our feet repeating the measures. The rest of the block was spent reviewing the beginning of the second movement, from dot seven, to put it musically on the move after dinner.

Dinner that evening was more peaceful for me. I ate my food quietly and quickly and went upstairs to the bandroom to doze off against the band lockers with the others for a half an hour. It was nice to have a little nap, but it was very uncomfortable. The doors on the lockers aren't solid; instead they consist of painful widely-spaced, little metal bars. *Next time,* I thought, *I'm sleeping on the floor.* Such activities aren't entirely uncommon in the land of Band.

The sun was creeping toward the tree line as cars pulled back into parking spaces and instruments emerged from cases once again. Feet shuffled rhythmically up and down the stairs. I yawned, slapping on my hat and stretching my legs. Ouch. Bad move. I looked down at my legs. Earlier I must have missed the backs of my legs putting sunscreen on, because they were now red and throbbed painfully every time I took a step or stretched.

I joined the other students outside, being careful not to take large steps. I wasn't the only one with a sunburn; several of the other girls' shoulders and faces were lobster red from the first two days of camp. At least we could all look forward to slathering soothing aloe vera gel on ourselves when we left band camp for the night.

The last two hours of band camp flew by. We rehearsed the music for about forty-five minutes in an arc with the pit and then took the field. Unfortunately, we couldn't get all the way to letter O on the move in the evening's rehearsal; it needed at least another day's work. However, conquering only the subsets for the night was nothing to be ashamed of. Most of the other schools started their band camp earlier, and they only lasted one week instead of two.

Later, everyone compared sunburns and raccoon-eyes. My brother had an especially funny set of 'coon-eyes from his oddly shaped sunglasses. (School pictures were the next Monday and Tuesday at registration. I'm sure many of the parents weren't happy about those pictures…)

I thought the horn line had it tough, lugging around heavy metal instruments, but as we put together all of our parts on the field, I began to notice everyone else. The pit had large instruments that had to be taken to the bandroom by elevator with the help of about half the horn line, and about fifty different pairs of mallets and drumsticks to keep track of. The drum line worked with their techs Rob and Tyrone, practicing all day with heavy drums hanging on their backs and shoulders.

Even the guard had a tough routine; not a single member of an audience (without experience) gave them proper credit for the work behind the beauty and the smiles. Every flag pole is weighted and prone to tugging from the wind. The rifles and sabers smack their hands and wear out their arms for the sake of an amazing visual. And our poor drum majors who kept their cool even when we weren't completely following directions deserved applause!

Overall, the musical section provided a good place to start next time: we would be tackling letter O for the first time on the field. We managed to use some of the new attacks and dynamics in the holds, and although it really need more work, we were making astounding progress. Before we were released from Padawan, it was made known that our homework was to start memorizing movement three of our show: the ballad.

As the sun was slowly setting, I climbed into Dominick's black truck with my brother, leaned against the seat, closed my eyes, and finally relaxed.

I can do this. We can do this.

There would be no frustrated tears on my face and no doubts in my mind that night (or any other night) for the rest of the season.

Chapter 4: Like a Wildfire

Band Camp Days 4 & 5- July 28-29, 2011

"It's been a long, hot week, and we didn't know what the heck we were doing, but hey, it was fun." remarked Maddie Trelz, a clarinet player.

We scrambled to stay afloat at the rigorous pace Padawan established this week. Work hard, work harder, then double it. Repeat.

It didn't help that we had two more holes: a senior clarinet player, Belle, was moving, and a sophomore tenor saxophone-player, Brad, had nerve damage in his shoulder.

Towards the end of the season, I got a chance to ask him how he had felt.

"At first I was really disappointed. I was pretty mad, but there wasn't really anything I could do about it… I did like all the free time, though, because Marching Band takes a *lot* of time, every day. I got used to it."

One of our color guard members, Skyler, was also injured and on crutches.

Already we were starting to feel the heat, and the pressures of a long and tough season ahead were starting to rise. Tensions among us were getting slightly hot on the field. For the most part it was difficult but fun under the sun, given the exception of a few sections with discord.

Prior to the start of band camp, sections were directed to hold sectionals (small meetings to just hang out and work on marching or music) often, but more play was involved than work. After all, we were teenagers. Apparently some of us could not follow peers because of similar age, or for contradicting feelings and beliefs about the group.

Band is, like many professional and educational

institutions, very political. It's a democracy, a dictatorship, and a system of hierarchy all at once. Padawan, the School Board, and the Band Parents Association (BPA) were like the checks and balances system in the government. Padawan was the president, the BPA was his Congress, and the School Board was his Supreme Court. If Padawan decided something- for example, that our end-of-year trip would be to go to Disney World- first the BPA needed to approve or disapprove, then a budget estimate would be made, the trip would be organized, and the School Board would finally give their approval or disapproval. This is the way most school groups function.

Within the band, Mr. Padawan was in charge, and openly asked for our opinions and suggestions from time to time. Sometimes he put his foot down and said "no," "yes," or "do it." Other times, things were quite flexible. Students were allowed to demonstrate leadership not only through the official Leadership Team, but also through organizing fundraisers and helping set up before concerts.

The way marching band currently ran was effective, and most were okay with student-run sections, or they kept their gripes to themselves. The lone guy in the clarinet section for the year, Miguel Gonzalez, otherwise known as "Sheep," smiled when I asked him what he thought. "It's okay to me. I mean, if I was a senior and a freshman was in charge of my section, I would have no problem with it as long as they deserved the job."

Other students had a more ambitious view of it. The other "new" flute, Rachel, shrugged. "It's…okay. I don't mind. Yeah, next year, I want a shot at leadership. But I don't mind students running the sections as long as, say, a trumpet leader or one of the saxophone leaders isn't bossing other sections around."

Our flute and clarinet sections were on our own on the field, since being a drum major came first to our section leaders. "It was really hard and stressful." said Molly. "I had to pick between being section leader and fixing things and being drum major. There's no way I can do both at once- except for running sectionals outside of band, that is."

Band was also like a family. In tough times, we grew stronger and closer together. And, like every family, it had its moments when everyone wanted to strangle one another out of frustration, be it for lack of communication or lack of consideration, or for any other reason.

It was almost impossible to not be like another family. There's a true saying we used that explains how close we were: You know you're a band geek when you see your section more than your own family. It's because in band, *everyone fits in somehow.* We're all pieces to the puzzle.

On Thursday morning we learned the box drill in basics. It combined all of our forward, backward, left, and right slides into a figure-eight double box. There were nearly collisions in different rows when someone accidentally missed a direction change or went too fast or too slow. If basics were *this* hard, marching on the field would bring even greater challenges.

After the grueling box drill exercises, we worked on running through the whole show, from the top to the end of movement two, which we had set previously in the morning; we even played on the move up to letter O.

Before running our drill and setting new dots, Padawan had an announcement to make. "Guys, we have two more holes now. It's not good. Brad here has a shoulder problem, and we lost a clarinet player from our program." He paused. Poor Brad looked kind of upset, sitting over at the front sideline watching us, his tenor sax on his lap. "But there's good news as well. Brian Munoz, our alternate, has agreed to march tenor sax instead of flute to maintain the shape of the formations. He'll have to relearn dots and carry something a *lot* heavier than a flute. Give him a round of applause!" We all burst into loud cheers and hollers, watching Brian blush.

"Thanks for trying, Brad. Go get that shoulder fixed."

Now we were back to four on-field flutes. Two freshmen signed up, but never showed up, which was a problem. The band has a paid drill writer every season who takes both the music and our numbers into consideration and creates our formations. Since the two non-existent members had spots written into the drill, we had two holes to fill to complete each picture.

On Friday, Danielle Maggio, a freshman flute player, showed up and joined us, leaving only one flute hole. Across the ensemble, we now had only four holes; unless they were filled, they would disappear from the formations for the last three movements of the show.

By lunch-time of Thursday, every dot of movement two and part of movement three was on the field. The positivity was catching from student to student like the twenty-four-hour flu. Over lunch break, after witnessing a dance created by the mellophones to signal that they had found their dots and were waiting on everyone else, the flutes and clarinets decided to make a dance.

We spent no time practicing over lunch. Instead, we argued about what our dance should involve. What later became our "hoop" dance evolved from a *long* discussion involving "sagging", the hula, hula-hooping, and minimizer shorts.

Molly wouldn't budge from her idea that the dance should involve hula-hooping. Trevor and Miguel suggested that it would look silly if they did it and refused to try. Staci hopped up and started to hula-hoop with air. The rest of us stared; nobody told us that band camp made everyone crazy!

Eventually, all the girls agreed to it, ignoring Trevor's and Miguel's protests. "Go dance with the mellos. Traitors."

Either way, our dance was established. By the time we rehearsed the formations later in the evening, we were hoopin'.

Molly and Staci began to spend more time together, organizing all of the sectional-parties for the week between band camp and school, and designed the section shirts. Nearly all of the two sections' members followed suit and intermingled during the days that were slowly slipping by. Band camp was almost halfway over.

After eating and dancing through lunch, Padawan got us on the move again (after showing us how to do the *real* breathing gym, of course). Before, he had only showed us how to do a part of our breathing exercises. It takes more than the average percent of lung capacity used for walking or playing an instrument while sitting, and we didn't yet have the endurance or practice to sustain loud volumes, high notes, or the fast tempos that *Solaris* would demand us to perform. It was time to push ourselves even further.

By now, all the members joked about Padawan strolling out each day wearing dark sunglasses and an intense look on his face. It was the *playtime's over, time for work* look.

He strolled out, set his cooler in the center of the circle next to him, and cleared his throat, clapping his hands to get our attention. "Welcome back. It's not so hot this afternoon, is it? We've all had a nice lunch break, finished movement two and set the first four dots of movement three earlier. We're off to a great start, guys. Let's keep it up." He paused. "Yesterday, we began to learn breathing gym. Today, we'll do more of that and work on our attacks and holds in the first and second movement. Okay, warm up on your own."

I stretched before fingering through scales. The backs of my legs were still a light-reddish brick color from the previous day's sunburn. *Owwww....*

The breathing exercise we learned wasn't too difficult, although it was mildly tiring. First, we breathed in and out for decreasing lengths of time, which helped us prepare for the next level.

It was an interesting exercise. For four counts we sucked in as much air as possible and then took small sips of air for several more counts to completely fill our lungs. Then, in one gush, we released the air, starting with a steady stream and then ending with a raspy hiss to empty our lungs. This whole process was followed by a deep breath in and then a big sigh. It might seem odd or unusual, but it helped a lot. Marching takes a lot of air on its own, and so do high notes. The more prepared we were to endure this season's demands, the better and easier the season would be.

The rest of the day ran smoothly, and the sun set on a bunch of sweaty but smiling sunburned faces. We found the renewed energy to storm upstairs and run to the band lockers, grab our gym bags and heavy cases, and run back to the empty cars and parents waiting for us in the parking lot.

Friday morning I woke to a bright beam of light streaming through my window. Unlike the other days, I actually had time to get ready instead of choking down my breakfast and leaving in a hasty rush.

Beneath the damp mask of sunshine, the air was fresh and sweet. There was spring in our steps as we entered the band room and prepared for rehearsal. The echoing pops of cases swinging open and sporadic giggles spilled out into the hallway, where several members were eating a quick breakfast. The "breakfast of champions" for some was Pop-Tarts; for others, it was a breakfast meal from McDonald's.

The morning went faster than any other in the week. We were accustomed to the heat and got used to the marching in between water breaks. There were no extra breaks, and the block was just as long. We were just getting used to surviving.

Basics were the same: box drill, factory, step size exercises. It became painfully obvious which marchers were veterans and which marchers were the newbies. Not all "newbies" were bad marchers; several showed the real promise of excellence. Others, like me, were getting there...eventually.

Padawan called us all to gather around him after basics for an announcement. Danielle showed up, so there was only one more flute hole. The clarinets and trumpets still had one hole each. We listened eagerly as he cleared his throat and looked at us. "It was inevitable that we would have a couple holes. We had someone move, people had quit, there was a medical case. We couldn't avoid it, and we're down to three holes, two of which will be filled today." That was a surprise. So we were going to gain two marchers *after* Danielle showed up? Incredible!

"Two of your drum majors, Molly and Staci, have agreed to act as marchers for the first two movements and then exit the field and direct for the remainder of the show to fill those spaces. This is both a huge sacrifice and an honor. Give both of them a round of applause!" We clapped and cheered wildly, seeing them smile and blush.

Later on, when I asked both Molly and Staci how they felt getting to march *and* direct as drum majors, they smiled and said they were lucky to do both and wouldn't have it any other way. "It's the best of both! What a way to start the season!" And for the rest of the season, we continued to feel whole, instead of feeling *full of holes*.

After circle drill and musical block in the afternoon, we hit the....pavement. The janitors were aerating the field with large machines, so we moved everything out to the parking lot to serve as a field for the evening block.

The horn line was out in the lot in an arc long before the pit equipment rattled all the way out to the "sideline". Echoes of the sound of us warming up bounced off the face of the gymnasium in front of us and hit us like a brick in the face.

Dominick and Jordan tested the met and the speakers. The faint echoes created after each downbeat promised to mess up our timing and attack strength as an ensemble. It was an inconvenient situation, but tolerable for the day.

The pavement brought new problems (*Oh my gosh-where are the lines? I can't look where I'm going! There are no hashes, I'll never find my dots!!!*) and a reality-check. Lumpy fields of grass wouldn't hold us back on turf (astro-turf for *fancy* stadiums) but it would be no advantage if we, the new guys, continued to rely on the hashes for each move. You couldn't really look where you were marching. You had to *know*.

Over the past few field rehearsals, Padawan began to call out names and address individual problems. My name was called more than a few times, events my brother harped about over our late night snacks after we got home each night. Apparently, I was an embarrassing marcher. (I am happy to say that that wasn't the case at the end of the season.)

The position of the lift gave a new perspective to the things that poised unnoticed before, like one of the small circle formations involving the saxophones. Maryn, the bari sax-player, kept over-shooting one of her dots in a formation and caught Padawan's eye.

"Maryn, you're too far. Move over." "Maryn, move to your right." A few dots later, Padawan called her name again. "Maryn, you're all over the place here. You're like a *wildfire* going out of control. Try adjusting your step size." From that day on, it became a motivational phrase. Every time we mentioned it, Maryn cracked a grin. "Heck yeah! I *feel* like a wildfire!"

During the evening field block, we debuted our dance for the very first time. Mr. Padawan was checking our dots and had already okayed the woodwind formations. Molly and Staci looked at each other. Staci, cupping her hands, called to us softly, "Hoop!" (This was the signal for our dance.) As we all pretended to reach down, pick up a hula hoop, and dance, Mr. Padawan stopped calling dots. He squinted down at us. "What are you guys doing? It looks like you're....hula hooping? Looks like we've got a dance competition among the sections!" Everyone chuckled when the mellophones joined in with their dance and the tubas bobbed up and down. "Okay. Quit dancing. Go find your next dot."

We were undeniably on fire. There were a few disappointing moments here and there, but we gave it our best. Padawan's parting remarks that Friday night, aside from reminding us to practice, praised our efforts and expressed the pride he had in us.

"You guys...you guys are awesome! Your effort and dedication to marching band is incredible. I know it's been hot and long, but you guys are doing *so* well. If we keep up this pace, we'll blow all the competition clear out of the water. Okay. You guys deserve a break. Go home, eat, go to sleep. Go for a jog sometime this weekend to keep in shape, or be prepared for a brutal Monday morning. Taking a whole weekend off will make it all the harder to get back into gear. Don't forget to practice. You're dismissed. See ya later."

Oddly, quite the opposite of the receding sunset, my energy was *electric*. I ran both up to the band room and back toward Dominick's car with all of my stuff. I waited impatiently for everyone to catch up.

That night, both Zach and I had a late night snack in the kitchen. I asked him how he felt about the last few days.

"It's going good, just wait till next week." *Crunch, crunch.* "Wait until body day. *That's* the fun part." *Crunch, crunch.* "Ready to quit yet?"

"No," I said. "This is awesome. I can't believe I made it this far. I won't be watching everyone else marching football half-time shows. This time, I'll be a part of it."

I thought about the last few days and how much I was already learning. By the end of the season, I would have the whole nearly ten-minute show memorized, people would watch us march, and we'd have body movements and horn moves while playing. I felt a shudder run through me. *Performance. Yikes.*

And then I remembered, *I've got all my friends behind me. We're going to be unstoppable.*

Chapter 5: Surface of the Sun

Band Camp Days 6 & 7- August 1 & 2, 2011

I squeezed my eyes shut. My alarm clock was chirping at me to get up.

Ugh. I rubbed my eyes with the back of my fist as I slowly slid from beneath my covers and sat up.

"GOOD MORNING, BAND! GOOD MORNING!"

Yeah, yeah. I had done nothing but sit inside my air-conditioned house the whole weekend. How difficult it was to go outside and stand in the sun!

The weatherman promised high temperatures and bright skies. Unfortunately, he was right on the mark. It wasn't nearly as hot as last Tuesday, but it was certainly hotter than any of us would like. I was envious of my younger sister, who had access to a pool and the air conditioning all day, while we were sweating to death.

My friend Liz agreed with me that mornings were certainly the worst. "It's ok, Katy. The competitions are fun. You'll like rehearsals more later on."

Every seasoned band member I talked to (except my brother, and it was because he *was* my brother) had nothing but reassuring and positive comments for new members. Many of the older members who could drive and had their freedom took freshmen to get dinner or invited them to hang out. I was stunned how fast everyone else was bonding. Everyone talked to everyone and nobody was really excluded.

It became apparent that nicknames are inevitably created in sections. Some of them poke fun at marching skills or memorable events and others involve last names. Among the more memorable are: Noodles, Shoe, Wildfire,

Kirby, Sheep, Frooba, Fish, Marshmallow, “R”, {untitled}, Princess, Smalls, Big John, Schmitstain, Chief, the Three Bears, Mr. Tinkles, and Period Nose. (Don’t judge- we’re band kids!)

Silly or embarrassing, nobody means any harm by the names. The nicknames are intended to bring everyone together, like secret passwords for members of a club.

We’re all on this journey together. We sweat together, work together, laugh together, and achieve together.

And right at the moment, we were roasting together.

The sun’s effect on us was just as awful as it was last Tuesday when we first stepped outside for morning exercises, if not worse. At least half of us (by my guess) were lazy all weekend and felt the brutality of the heat amplified by the lack of conditioning. After only ten minutes outside, I was seriously regretting not going for a jog either Saturday or Sunday.

Much to Mr. Padawan’s disappointment, a few of us had to sit out during morning rehearsal. This added to the craziness of the day’s schedule; not only were we losing people to week-long vacations and family reunions, but also to the school registration taking place in the first two days of the week.

We took our time with basics and water breaks, since any progress made would have to be repeated when everyone returned anyway. At least we managed to clean up our techniques significantly in spite of the heat. Our step sizes were greatly improved from last week, which redeemed us after slacking over the weekend.

After a longer water break (about three minutes long), we hit the field for the fourth movement. Movement three was almost completely set by Friday, but not fully run with music. We started the drill block with the last four dots of movement three and ran it once- *boom, boom, boom, done!*

"Ok. Standing where you are, everyone turn around. Wave at Molly."

Molly smiled and waved from the top of a metal stepladder set up at the center of the back sideline.

"Most of movement four will be marched facing backfield." Several seniors cheered. Padawan ignored it and explained the turn-around move to us step by step. Basically, we would watch Kayla to cut off the hold and give us two downbeats counting "One, two…" and then the normal four counts ("Turn"- plant left foot sideways, turning- "Turn," –repeat with right- "Lock" {now facing backfield}, "Push," finally bringing the right foot around to normal position) and the downbeat when we step out.

We repped this addition several times before continuing through the new movement. In sets of four we slowly made our way through the pinwheel set (I was the center of the far left pinwheel from the audience's perspective), the line sets, and all the way to the march across the field to the triple-circle formation, where things became very interesting for us.

"Go take another water break. You guys are working so hard; I'm very impressed. After the break, reset to your current dot and put down your first chip."

We scurried to the sideline and back, refreshed. Nothing tastes as good as water to an athlete working hard.

It's really unfair, but most other athletic groups snub marching band and its members by refusing to accept it as a sport. Technically, it is; we learn advanced marching techniques and train and perform to compete. We love it. We sweat for hours in the sun during the hottest days of the summer and every single day of the week after school except for Fridays. We have a combination of talent and skill to aid us on the field like any athletic group, and I can even boast arm and leg muscles I never thought I had due to the rigorous exercises.

I can't stress enough how upset band members who wish to take athletic Physical Education (a weight-training and workout version of gym class for *athletes* and the athletically gifted with extra cardio sessions) feel when they try to sign up and are told, "Sorry, you're not in a *sport*. You can't take this class." If anything, it takes *years* and years of extra skills to play an instrument well on the move from memory, let alone marching with the straight-leg technique we use, in difficult formations, and taking the class would help train the members better and condition muscles to prevent injuries. Not everyone can perfect a backwards eight-to-five or catch a quadruple rifle spin. (The day someone can gather twenty random athletes and have them execute an acceptable marching or flag routine or correctly without training and in time is the day we will believe we are not athletes.) Without the benefit of the more intense athletic gym classes, the students who carry the heaviest instruments (weighing anywhere from ten to thirty-plus pounds) must often begin the season physically unprepared. Better training and preparation offered through the athletic gym classes would prevent more muscular injuries on the field.

Back on the field, we set the next dots and returned to our places. (Without the chips to help us learn where to go, we wouldn't be nearly this far.) Yawns jumped from player to player; the heat was making some of us sleepy and it wasn't quite time for lunch (and the temptation of a nap afterward).

"Ok, it looks like everyone's already set. This next dot- go find it, quickly, and drop your next chip there- you will turn and face whichever direction you move." Mr. Padawan patiently watched us as we set the next chip. "Ok. The same rule applies for the next dot. Go find it."

After finding all of our dots for the double circle and running the new moves several times, it began to feel like a little whirlwind. We all swirled from a bigger circle toward the middle like a swarm of bees to a hive and then shot backward out in all directions before turning to finally face the front for a hold.

All this was accomplished by the time lunch rolled around. Some of the formations looked crooked and the lines a bit curvy, but we had a large chunk of movement four on the field. It was certainly something to be proud of, being a few days ahead of other bands and still going strong. Each day our intonation was noticeably improving, as was volume. We weren't at the pretty quadruple-forte cap we expected quite yet, but at that rate we worked, I believed we could learn to shake the stars with our sound and rattle the big bright ball of gas our show paid tribute to.

Throughout Monday and Tuesday afternoon, students disappeared from the field to go clean up, find their parents for school registration, and take school I.D. pictures.

Those photographs go in the yearbook as well as on the student identification cards, so they are considered to be a big deal. I imagine many parents were not amused or happy with the pictures they bought of raccoon-eyed, sunburned kids. *Anyone up for retakes?*

After lunch, we practiced circle drill; volume and timing, as well as complicated direction changes that were the keys to unlocking our potential on the field. The sooner we started to apply them in the show, the better.

The sun relaxed its grip on the earth in the later hours of the day, creeping through clouds and sinking steadily toward the horizon line like a gleaming golden spoon dipping to stir distant skies and release the stars for the night. Mosquitoes that lurked in the shadows during the day emerged in the dusk and began to bite, irritating our sweating skin further.

I wish I had remembered bug repellant spray. At least the few people with the worst sunburns in the group didn't seem to be getting bitten- the thought of itchy bites on top of painful burns seemed pretty awful! And apparently, this has been a mild bug year…

Before Padawan released us, at 8:00 sharp- after we rehearsed with the pit, ran the first three movements all together, and put the first few measures of movement four on the move musically, he cautioned us to keep ourselves hydrated.

"Listen up. Guys- I can't do everything for you. I can make sure you exercise and drink water here, but I can't go to your houses and remind you to drink water later. You sweat out most of the liquids you have on the field, and to catch up, you need to drink extra water. Stay hydrated tonight, and drink some water with your breakfast tomorrow morning, or else you'll feel sick and have to sit out. We can't have people getting sick because they don't take care of themselves. Okay? Go home. Drink water and *sleep*."

The next morning- Tuesday, the seventh day of band camp- fared better. Basics block went remarkably smoother, being that the air had cooled from Monday and a mild breeze drifted in. It was going well until we got on Padawan's nerves when people kept asking to go to the bathroom in the middle of rehearsal.

Clearly, he was a bit frustrated when he next addressed us. A few people, he suspected, defied the unforgiving no-milk-for-breakfast policy.

"Dudes- I've told you before: come prepared for the day. *If you drink milky-poo with your breakfast-poo, then you're going to go poo-poo.*" He said this in the ridiculous way he talks when addressing errors in common sense, an icky-sweet tone of voice with equally silly gestures in accompaniment. "Don't be stu."

Some of us raised our eyebrows. He explained early on in band camp that the phrase, "don't be stu" doesn't mean he thinks us stupid or incapable; we're band kids, for crying out loud, amongst the smartest kids in the bunch at high school. *However*, intelligence does occasionally take a vacation, and it has its own term, "being stu," which applies when we don't follow explicit instructions or we make foolish choices.

Around us, Padawan wasn't the "high and mighty band director." He was one of us, but with more authority. If something needed handled or addressed, he did so as the situation required; more often than not, minor events required the humor equivalent to that of the person being corrected. Firmly, of course, but with enough humor to earn a short batch of chuckles and encourage a more positive reaction with more success than yelling or push-up punishment would.

Everyone laughed at the end of the speech. I think

it received the intended response and stuck in our memory a lot longer, with no offense taken at being "stu."

It's just the way band works. Humor (at the appropriate times) packs a more powerful punch in marching band, and it's not a one-way street, either. Every year, around Thanksgiving, the school held either a pie, spaghetti, or pudding "pig out" contest for teachers and students to win money. The ten students and ten teachers with the most money donated to their container had to compete to eat a moderate portion of food the fastest. Padawan absolutely *hated* being put in the competition, but we had done it since his first year here and planned to continue doing it. It was funny, especially because he came nowhere close to winning, and the whole band cheered him on anyway. (We were very loyal, be it a good or bad thing!) Watching your band director stuffing his face with spaghetti was the way many chose to get even after the season for a good laugh.

The basics block was a lot tougher this morning. To make up for the indoor "Body Day" scheduled for the next day, when we would learn dance moves for the opener, we rehearsed *everything* we've learned on the field. Box drill, volume control, factory, and anything else that could possibly build our skills: we practiced it all for a good part of the morning.

While we rehearsed outside in the morning, guard instructor Alyssa drilled the color guard and taught the girls their routines for the show, including the solos in the third and fifth movements, as well as the various flag and rifle features scattered throughout the show. Her sandy-blonde ponytail bobbed as she demonstrated a spin for Leah, a sophomore dancer who would perform the dance solo in the third movement. Alyssa was liked by everyone for her sense of humor and because she was really good at what she did.

Later, the guard would join us for the field rehearsal block so we could put all the new parts of the show together. The most important part of learning drill is keeping up with the rest of the show and being able to put catch up at the end of the day with *everything* on the field.

After resetting the circle dots and running through the backwards and forwards moves into the huge thirty-two count hold body section, we were dismissed, and stormed the cafeteria for food (staying on our half of the room so we wouldn't disrupt school pictures). Lunch was my favorite part of each day, no argument there. An hour and a half to chill or goof off was perfect to replenish energy spent in the morning exercises.

When we dragged our water and towels and instruments outside for circle drill, reluctant to leave the air-conditioned building, someone noticed and commented on our director's t-shirt. Looking at it, Padawan smiled and recited the story of the Carolina Crown horn line's "Honey Badger" t-shirts.

"Be the Honey Badger." A short nature lesson: a honey badger is a fearsome little beast. It's a badger that will stop at nothing to get food and can eat (and survive bites from) venomous snakes. It's fast and vicious, but most importantly, *nothing* stands in its way. Therefore, if we were to be determined like the honey badger, then nothing would stop us. (Yes, yes, those clarinet players were like the honey badger- not only were they talented and dedicated, but they could also be vicious! Just joking.)

What's stopping me? My fear of performance was

going to be a tough challenge to face, like many of the fresh faces around me. *Am I afraid of my dots?* No. I'm going to *eat* my dots! All of us were beginning to seek to devour our dots one by one and emerge triumphant in neat formation. It was that hunger for achievement, striking down our doubts and reaching for accuracy and improvement, which was slowly and surely changing the season. Into what, I could not tell then; but at that moment, affirmed by the progress made throughout the musical rehearsal and evening block, I knew *Solaris* was going to take us to the edge and test our limits. If we could prepare enough and rise to that challenge, then this would truly be *our* year. Truly, we would live up to the title of our high school, "The High School of Champions."

I thought about this the rest of the day. The road ahead loomed long and intimidating, but not impossible. *We can do this.*

But first, we would have to learn how to dance.

Chapter 6: Tribal

Band Camp Day 8- August 3, 2011

You know it's going to be an interesting day when all the music learned over the past few days keeps playing in your head like a broken record, non-stop, and you can't help but finger along with your part in the air. And then, to accompany the memorable music, there would be a catchy little dance to practice. (People are definitely going to stare if anyone gets bored in public and starts to hum and dance!)

Other band kids found their thoughts consumed by dots and technique as well. Several freshmen joked that they practiced eight-to-five steps for fun in their yards and down their streets. Others played the catchy musical lick (band slang for a run of notes or an easily recognizable phrase that usually requires a lot of skill) at letter O in the second movement as fast as they could to show off in the mornings and during meal breaks.

Band kids are just amazing like that.

Upon arriving at school, we hurried up to the band room. The excitement was just *killing* some of us! Of course, the seasoned members had gotten dance moves and performed before, but to the newer members, it was really cool. Last year, in the show *Rhythms of a City*, the entire band had a hip-hop dance that looked *amazing*. Everyone moved together like a giant, rippling wave of purple and black amid the gleaming mirrors on our shakos ("shako" is the official term for our "marching hats".) That one dance began my marching envy that led me to my current place, F3.

While practicing on the field, and this morning in the auditorium where we were going to rehearse the body movements for the first two movements, we wore our loose athletic shorts and shirts, comfortable tennis shoes, and baseball hats or sunglasses. In performance, we had to do all the moves with a tall plume on each shako, restrictive marching uniforms, and rigid black marching shoes. It all looks nice, but any band member will tell you that it does affect the difficulty of the show for the individual.

One of the ideas about marching (and parade) band that drove us crazy was when people call our shakos "hats". It especially drove Molly crazy, and whenever someone slipped up and asked about our hats, she would quickly correct their mistake, "They're *shakos*!"

(Unless you want to face the wrath of a band student, do *not* call them hats.)

Up in the band room, at precisely 9:00, Padawan raised his hands for silence. "Alright, here's the plan: we'll take instruments, towels, and waters down to the auditorium- stop moving around, please- and stretch on the stage. I'll meet you down there in five minutes. Line up the instruments by section in the front where they won't get stepped on. Okay, go."

The cool air escaping from the airconditioned auditorium brushed our faces as we filed in through the glass double doors, passing the guard and drumline practicing on the concrete near the parking lot and outside the Fine Arts building. The color guard members were practicing drop-spins. Despite the lack of wind outside, the light flag-silks fluttered gracefully as if there was a breeze lifting them.

It was dark in the auditorium, except for the stage.

All the overhead lights were on, highlighting the faded brown room that was slightly noisy and halfway disorganized.

"Where's Molly?"

"Hey! Watch it!"

"Move!"

"No, we're over there. Don't set your instrument *here*." (Molly herding the newbies)

After about five minutes of confusion, we settled down and assembled into rows on the stage and 'spaced out' (standing at least arm's length apart- Padawan warned our section leaders to tell us that we would need plenty of space), not to say that some of us weren't already off in our own little worlds….

Just then, Padawan jogged into the auditorium and onto the stage smiling. "Sweet! You guys are all set and ready to go- awesome!" He clapped his hands together. "Okay, lets get started!"

His enthusiasm quickly infiltrated the group of energetic teenagers waiting to begin. We couldn't get done with our stretches soon enough; the moment we finished, groups shuffled around and traded for spots next to friends. Some of us took off our shoes and left them near our open cases off to the side of the stage, rehearsing "the body" (as we refer to it) in sock-feet.

We were so excited, it was *crazy*. Those of us who had known Mr. Padawan for a year or two knew he performed with *Blast!*, an *insane* performing musical group that was a bit heavier on "dancing" in their shows than normal marching band. With this in consideration, we expected a routine no less spectacular than last year's dance.

I wasn't worried, even though I'm not very

coordinated. The entire morning block, all three hours of it, was reserved for learning the opener, which was plenty of time. *I'm sure I'll get by the end of the week....*

Padawan raised his hand to quiet the whispering and shuffling. "Okay. So, after trying some different things…" He looked around at us, making eye contact, "I decided that we are going to start the show like *this*. Take a seat, please."

We sat down, surprised.

"Okay. Now, sit with your legs crossed, like this."

We giggled and whispered as we scooted around, adjusting to the strange position.

"Oh, come on. I'm old, and if I can do this, you should be able to."

Next, we were to sit up straight with our palms resting face-down on our knees and watch him for twenty-four counts, or two sets of twelve.

"On the second set of twelve, on beat eleven, be ready, because on beat twelve," he said, shifting slightly, "you'll take your right hand and, on the beat, stick your arm straight out to your right palm down. Then, with your arm still straight, fingertips flexed, lean forward slightly and make a circle. One-two-three, the arm will be in front moving across to your other knee, and four-five-six, going up above your shoulder. Good! Now flip your hand-gracefully, now seven-eight-nine, as it arcs around, ten-eleven, and ends almost back at your side, but palm-up. This is half of the move."

We practiced and repped the move and added in the other half (also in twelve counts, mirroring with the left side) for a total of twenty-four counts until they were almost fluid. A few times someone started with the wrong hand or missed the hand move on beat twelve and giggled.

Then the two halves of the group on the stage (split down the middle) competed for accuracy and bragging rights.

Casey Powers, one of the competitive sophomore clarinet players, showed others near her how to do the moves correctly. Soon the whole band wore a look of intense concentration, fighting to maintain focus and achieve perfection. An hour later, we were practicing the complete move.

When we were given the whole routine, it reminded us of some sort of ancient ritual. The movements of *Solaris* were meant to sound tribal (especially the percussion feature in the beginning of the show) and now we matched the music. Honestly, I was beginning to wonder, from the nature of the music, if any of the body moves called for offering a drummer as a sacrifice…

Whether fortunate or unfortunate, we were not instructed to grab any of the percussionists. Instead, after practicing the opener for about an hour and a half, we learned some horn and body moves for holds in the second and third movements.

For a hold near the end of movement three, the woodwinds had a twenty-four count hold and nothing to do while standing there. Since this movement was a flowing ballad, we were given a graceful "lean" to our right that we would hold until count twenty-one, up-up-lock and push for twenty-two, twenty-three, and twenty-four, with a step-out at twenty-five. Also, we received instruction for a "squat" move right before O in the second movement in twelve counts. "Left foot, to side; legs apart (triumphant) stomp one-two, squat for six, slide leg back for two, up-lock-*step-out*!"

After us, the brass received a horn move in their hold: horn down, foot out and lean, stretch- reach, a graceful hand movement back up with their trumpets, mellophones, or baritones, straighten, and push off.

That concluded the body block for the day.

After the band moms (and several dads) made hamburgers, nachos, and baked potatoes for lunch, many of us went upstairs or outside to sit down and practice the opener body moves. Like the challenging section at O in the second movement, it became one of the favorite group jam-session highlights; that is, we would wander around practicing our favorite memorized bits of the show, and if several band kids happened to group together, all would start to play O (the brass had their own spots they rehearsed that way) because we all knew it now. It was our own way of bragging that we put effort into it and learned it.

Upstairs, the flutes and clarinets took over the choir room per usual and sat down to apply sun lotion and work through the various rough patches in the music. Because several clarinets made the request, we skipped music and focused on counting the body until we mastered it. The clarinets really got into it, repeating it until they felt it looked clean and crisp enough with the timing.

Mr. Padawan had warned us that a photographer from a local newspaper was coming to photograph us during circle drill (and also during the morning dance tutorial). True to his word, a man from the newspaper hovered nearby snapping photos when we set a circle and held afternoon circle drill. The sunlight peering between large, drifting clouds gave our dusty instruments a dull shine that reflected onto our faces. We all tried not to follow the camera with our eyes, but it was difficult to focus on the exercise.

Later on, we all logged on to the website for the newspaper and laughed about the photos. Some were excellent and looked nice; others were more candid and kind of funny, snapped when someone was making a face or going cross-eyed looking over the bell of their instrument. Interestingly, there were few photos of Padawan. Apparently he hated having his picture taken.

Music rehearsal passed, then dinner break. It was a relief to sit at one of the polished lunch tables with the cool benches in the air conditioning and just think. I thought about the bet I made. Was it the only thing keeping me in the group? Or, was it fear of my parents' wrath if I quit and still had to pay the costly marching band fees?

No. Now, in the second week, after surviving the first, after finding that despite my doubts, I could *do* this- it was something else keeping me here. Something else was driving me, making me try my hardest and making me *care* about what happens on the field.

I looked around. Off the field we weren't ignoring each other, for the most part. When I walk upstairs each day, at least ten of my friends greet me along the way, and almost everyone knows each member's name in every section. As Mr. Padawan said, marching band guarantees many familiar faces on the first day and someone to sit with at lunch. Spending this much time together affects everyone: I was no exception.

I was here because of the team. I was here for my teammates. And I was here for me. I liked what this challenge was doing to me: making me stronger, more outgoing, and more skilled (not to mention more coordinated!).

Continuing the age-old tradition of choosing a freshman to be sponsored, or claimed as a "pet" as I called it, many upperclassmen chose band-mates as "their freshmen." This was one of the ways of extending the olive branch to the new kids and to make them feel that they had backup if they ran into trouble. I earned my nickname "Mom" because I always had bandages in my purse and I always talked to the freshmen to see how they're doing and made sure that they had friends to hang out with. "Sheep" the clarinet player was one of these, and little "freckles" Stahlman as well.

When we hit the field for the final rehearsal of the night and the sun slipped behind the buildings, I felt sad to leave. Moving through the music and across the field, weaving between other members and becoming part of the symphonic sound, feeling the depth of the music and being pulled along in a wave of emotional expression, we became something other than a rag-tag group of students. We forgot that everyone had issues, and became a majestic tide of power sweeping the field. We ceased to be individuals, and became a united ballad of light dancing in the dark and toward the final battle with the Goliaths of the Blue Division of GSL. Our size didn't matter, nor the fact that we couldn't stretch in formation all the way from ten-yard line to ten-yard line across the field like the huge bands with nearly one hundred and fifty members from neighboring competitors.

Now that I had lived and survived the first part of the season, even successfully learning my music and how to march (though still a work in progress), I had a lot of respect for my fellow band members and for myself. I was proud to be a part of this program, as proud as any student on any other athletic team would be of their program.

I was proud to be a member of my team, and anxious to see the season through to the end as a part of it.

The competitions couldn't come quickly enough for us. Nothing short of competing would sate our thirst for performance.

Chapter 7: Are We Done Yet?

Band Camp Days 9 &10 – August 4 & 5, 2011

The two weeks of band camp (and the extra weeks for guard and drum line) drew to a close quickly. Looking back, every member could name at least one thing they could take away from the experience. We learned how to avoid looking like lobsters or dehydrating in the Great St. Louis Oven (some of us learned faster than others). I believe the strongest lesson learned was work ethic: how to make good use of our time under the sun and in the company of our peers.

"It was very intense for me. Fun, but intense. I think it's really good preparation for the military or drum corps. I feel a lot stronger now than I was." -Stephen Rasp

"I learned how to sleep like a rock and I learned to sleep with ice packs when I got sunburned. Don't forget sun lotion. It sucks." – Maryn Kester

"It was hard work, but I feel great about it. And it was really fun. It put me in bed every night and got me out of it in the morning." – Maddie Trelz

Though many of us broke past our imagined limitations and became stronger, a few learned their limits off the field. A color guard member and percussionist, Kaitlynn Brown, discovered in the second week of band camp that she had a difficult breathing problem and couldn't stay outside in extreme heat. She would either have to quit or find something else to do.

"I thought, 'great, now what am I going to do?' and I was sad. Then Rob, who is in charge of pit and drum line, said that I would perform in the pit on the sideline. I just had to rehearse inside for most of the summer after switching," she recalled later on.

Seniors like Dominick had a different experience altogether. "I can't believe it's the last year I'll be out here on the field. It's weird and it kind of makes me sad to have to pass the torch on to the next section leader."

Freshman Miguel (A.K.A., "Sheep") agreed that the graduating class and incoming class interaction affected him as well. "Band Camp really helped with the transition into the high school because we were able to bond with the upper classmen and get to know everyone." As Padawan had said to us, being in band guarantees about a hundred familiar faces the first day of school, many of whom will share lunch periods and prevent the typical first day which-table-to-eat-at trauma. It was common to see clusters of band kids mixed with choir and non-band color guard members across the cafeteria each day during each lunch hour.

Early Thursday morning the band room was abuzz with excitement. The end of band camp was rapidly approaching. Some of us were torn between feelings of nostalgia and relief. School would start, then the football games, and then competitions, the first for many of us and the last for our seniors.

On the field in the morning drill block, we set the remaining dots of the fourth movement. Since it would be more efficient to clean the current set movements than to quickly learn a small part of five, Mr. Padawan decided that movement five would wait until school started. Therefore, the day was spent mainly on musical clean-up and polishing some of the sets, as well as solving problems in timing and tempo transitions.

"Do it again."

"Try again."

"One more time, from the top."

The same spots plagued us through the repetitions until we began to successfully incorporate the changes and perform consistently.

One of the changes we had to get used to was an alteration to the body in the opener. With our current routine, the saxophones had little time to get their saxes clipped back onto their neck straps. Padawan considered this after watching several times and cut out the last twelve counts of the body, changing it to allow extra time to increase the likelihood of success in performance. The change made the routine a little less complicated for everyone and erased the nervous looks from the saxophones' faces.

After lunch break, three exciting pieces of news were brought to our attention.

First, several band students got together and decided we were going to have a water balloon fight on Friday, the last day of band camp. Apparently we were going to be allowed to use a full-size trash can to hold the balloons and run around beaning each other with the wet projectiles during dinner break.

Also, directly after being soaked during dinner break, our evening rehearsals would be open to our families to watch as an unofficial "parent preview." (Padawan claimed that it was only for the sake of tradition, that it wouldn't really be anything special, we wouldn't be allowed to show off, and so on. Later on, it would prove otherwise when it became a notable occasion.)

What excited us the most, however, was news from the district and the school board. At the previous school board meeting, plans were submitted for review, voting, and potential execution for a "stadium." Between the lines, it meant a nice turf field to replace the sod mess we have and adding an extra set of "stadium seats" (standard metal bleachers). Only a suggestion, but now it was actually being considered. In the midst of economic troubles and unfair unbalances in funding from school district to school district, we caught a glimpse of hope for us. Unfairly, Collinsville was often snubbed by bigger, richer high schools with well-funded programs and expansive campuses and facilities. Our high school's nickname is "The High School of Champions," because in spite of the issues that plagued us and the smaller amount of money the school had to spend on its students, we managed to keep up with the other schools. The same could be said of our various sports and other performing arts programs; they, too, achieved beyond their means as we do.

This "stadium" (as it was referred to) was proof that our program was going to go somewhere new this year; I could feel it. The energy we spent on the field and off was going someplace we couldn't see, collecting and waiting for something incredible.

Over dinner break, while we recovered from the rigorous exercises involved in our daily ritual, the weather began to change. The overcast skies emptied the water they had hoarded for the past two weeks onto us and the field, eliminating any chances of us using the marshy grass to rehearse. Instead, we hit the parking lot. The rain lasted less than fifteen minutes in a drenching downpour, so we continued with the evening block under a blanket of clouds and cool air, the only lasting signs of a change in the weather pattern.

Evening block was genuinely exciting and fun. Once the dots were learned and the music was added, rehearsing became less of a boring experience and more of a delightful challenge. Sure, nobody particularly likes to repeat a small section eleven times in a row, but feeling the rush of adrenaline from the powerful, driving melodies and the intense footwork of a large section is well worth all the hard work involved in learning the dots.

The changes were gradual, but over the past few nights we ceased to drag ourselves outside to the cars like limp bags of bones, and marching while playing made practicing while standing still seem even easier. We now had the energy and strength to bring music to life on the field.

On Friday we would face our first (and perhaps second most stressful) performance: performing the four movements straight through for our families.

"Don't remind me! I'm gonna cry!" Molly exclaimed the next morning when we went outside for morning basics and rehearsal.

John only smiled at Molly, turned back to us in our crisp rows where we were sweating silently, and began his announcement.

"Hey, guys, this is it. Last day of band camp *ever* for seniors! Freshmen, you just survived your first band camp. Yeah!"

We all laughed and clapped loudly. Molly didn't cry, but she had a moist sparkle in her eyes a few times throughout the rehearsals. I could see similar sentiments with all the seniors there, expressed in a variety of ways-some more hidden than others, but definitely there.

The heat dropped to a tolerable eighty-five degrees with a muggy humidity stuck at ninety percent. Clouds rolled across the sky in clumps that periodically cast a shadow across our faces and shoulders as we spent the morning continuously cleaning and repping our formations and music.

After trampling the damp ground thoroughly, we headed inside for lunch. It was pizza day. Roughly thirty pizzas awaited us in four stacks of brown cardboard boxes that leaked their mouth-watering smells from within. We circled like a pack of hungry wolves.

Surprisingly, we didn't finish everything. That happened during dinner break when the Band Parents announced a free-for-all on the pizza leftovers. Cold, of course, but a pack of ravenous band kids will eat just about anything.

During circle drill, Mr. Padawan foreshadowed the embarrassment that would be felt if we forgot techniques because we would actually have an audience. "Don't wave at Mommy and Daddy while you're holding a note or during circle warm-up. Don't lose your focus just because you have an audience. Nothing should change from basics and rehearsals to the performance, unless it's *performing better than earlier.*"

Musical block seemed to pass slower than molasses in January. It was really hard to stand still and wait while other sections took their difficult parts "to the woodshed." (In band language, it means fixing at a lower tempo and working it up to tempo in small increments until it's fixed.) Everyone was waiting for the balloon fight and the Parent Preview.

Dinner finally came. The pizza disappeared within minutes.

It was forty minutes until the preview when word spread that Molly and a few others had filled an entire large lunchroom trash can with water balloons. About twenty members stormed outside noisily; the parents who were hanging out in the cafeteria with us only rolled their eyes.

The rule was, those who filled up balloons got dibs on taking the first shots, and everyone had to pick up the pieces afterwards. Molly, Nick, Staci, and the others carefully chose their arsenal. Then, after stepping back…

I shall not mention much about what followed, except that the concrete commons area outside next to the field was soaked and littered with balloon corpses, the staff and band director wisely chose to remain out of sight elsewhere on campus (probably safer that way!), and I had so much fun that I ended up dancing around in the chaos with someone else's camouflage hat, relatively dry and laughing. Not everyone was so lucky…

"I'll definitely miss driving the lift the most." –Jordan Olive

"I'll miss the food." (laughs) –Brian Munoz

"I'll miss the feeling of contentment after a hard day's work." –Melissa Simmons

"It was my last day of band camp. I'll miss being here with everyone!" –Dominick Viviano

"…" –Molly McClelland, who was fighting back tears and smiling

And, most concisely:

"Stuff." –Alfredo Deleon

I didn't list most of the amusing comments from the drummers about their basics, which were very detailed and… imaginative, yet ambiguous. Sorry, guys. But I'll always remember that drum line basics are (and I quote): "like getting shot in the mouth, then coming back to life like BAM!" –Weston, Jamie, Bigtyme, and Devon.

After all the waiting, I assumed the evening block would take forever.

"Welcome, Collinsville Band Parents and families, to the annual Parent Preview. It's been a great two weeks of really hard work. These kids have accomplished so much. Give them a hand."

It wasn't *that* hard. Not now, anyway. *If* I *of all people could do it, anyone can.*

Padawan turned his attention to us. We received spot-check instructions and repped certain parts of different movements, like the transitions between movements and arriving at holds in formation without blunders.

Kayla was a pro now at flipping the pages of her binder with her foot while directing and occasionally checking the met with the other. The sun was barely visible, so she wasn't wearing her usual pair of angled shades. Instead, you could see her eyes, clearly visible against her freckles, watching the mass of marchers.

"I was so proud of you guys," she told us later. "You guys worked hard and you stayed together and were all watching. I'm glad I didn't let you guys down."

The air was muggy; the field, buggy and a bit squishy. I could see several people filming us as we performed.

Near the very end of rehearsal, before the final run-through of the four movements we had learned and practiced on the field, we spent time working on the last dots of four that we had learned just the day before. Sections F and G were trouble spots; aside from having ridiculous musical runs, the approach to each dot was at such a slight angle forward for the majority of us that we often overshot the dots and finished too far forward.

We had just completed a rep and were about to run it again when a mellophone player, Courtney Griffith, fell and twisted her ankle in one of the low spots in the field right next to me. Several techs rushed over from the side of the field.

Luckily, it wasn't serious. The small audience cheered when Courtney stood up with bleary eyes and resumed her standby pose.

This time, we were lucky. Next time, it might be a broken ankle or leg.

The rest of the rehearsing was uneventful. Padawan announced our first performance, sent us back to our positions at the very first dot, and clicked off the mic.

The next moments flew by in a dizzying rush. It's difficult to find the right words to describe what it feels like to have adrenaline shoot from your feet, up through your stomach, and climb up your throat as you watch your drum major with bugged-out eyes, hardly daring to look away for the first counts. Then, suddenly the whole world seems to shift and spin as marchers move around you, and you follow, aware of *everything* around you. There isn't time for much thought process; raw emotion and determination consume your thoughts, shuffling out as quickly as your feet arrive at each new set. And, when you finally freeze in the final set, holding some apocalyptic note and straining to keep time with the drum major instead of your hammering heart and racing pulse, at last cut off- with the gasping breath that comes right after, and the tidal wave of pent-up nerves and excess energy crashing over you that sinks to your feet, you know the secrets of music, and why you live and breathe for it.

It was the feeling of a champion. Whether or not we took McKendree, Lafayette, or GSL- if we did our best, and pushed the limits as a team, then regardless of our scores and ranking, we *would* be champions. Our feelings would be our judgment, and our prize would be our memories.

We left the patchy field tired and relieved. It was a good start to the season, all the seniors admitted that.

There would be no rehearsals until a week later when school starts. Our success would depend upon retaining the skills and information we learned in band camp. If anything slips during the time off…we're going to be in hot water.

However, we had the confidence that we would do well to remember over the break…

"It had seemed like it would be fun, and awesome. It was." –Phil Collins

"I wasn't sure how this season would begin…I mean, last year was great. But camp really surprised me. I can't wait to see where this goes." –Sarah Court

I can't wait to see where this goes.

Part 2: Sunburn

Chapter 8: Whirl

The first rehearsal after a week off, when school began for the year, was absolutely *brutal*. Few of us had listened to Padawan's order to exercise over the break, and now we were paying for that mistake.

We were all a little off our game- the first full day of school always feels terrible. And then add on an intense circle drill, resisting mouth muscles, and hot temperatures after readjusting to air conditioning. The result: one miserable batch of students.

The weirdest feeling was the lack of response from leg muscles. The lumpy field suddenly felt unfamiliar and even more mountainous than before. Even worse, our postures drooped from the shoulders down and our instruments flopped around as we moved at unacceptable angles.

Yikes.

It was going to take some serious work to recover from the time off.

There was some good news. Padawan was excited despite our disappointing start for the week "Good news, guys: we're going to get a new student from Granite City. Luckily for us, she plays clarinet. She'll be here tomorrow. Her name is Krista, and she's excited to learn the show and help us out by filling a hole."

The clarinets looked considerably happier.

"She has already learned most of the Granite City show, so she will have to learn ours and work hard at the music. Everyone give her a warm welcome when she arrives tomorrow."

Meanwhile, the color guard was practicing drop spins on the concrete near the doors to the main school building.

"Five, six, five-six-seven-eight!" Silk twirled rapidly in glorious wheels of purple like supercharged fans. Alyssa clapped her hands, keeping the spins in time and watching with a keen eye.

The flags were having a better rehearsal than us, because unlike the horn line, they had sectionals several times throughout the week and had retained their learned routines well. Expectations were high- the girls were aiming to top their previous seasons and glide ahead of the competition. In fact, several were sure that this year was going to be better than any of the past seasons in the two years with Mr. Padawan.

Though this year had only a handful of girls in the color guard, the tightly-knit group was focused, dedicated, and ready to roll.

Later in the week, after particularly intense daily circle drills and considerable improvement in our stamina and first two movements of the show, it was time to clean up the ballad.

Both the guard and the drum line joined us on the field. Running the movement set to set, then in chunks, we were moved, fixed, or rearranged often to sharpen the formation. Sections were run first without instruments, then with the instruments, mostly air-only and then moving with music. Over and over again, we marched to memorize our dots and to get consistent results.

Embarrassingly enough, my name was one of those called periodically to be moved into the correct spot. I could practically feel the glaring looks from my brother burning into my back.

It was the end of the week before all of the third movement was cleaned up with flags and instruments. Each day, something we had fixed the day before was forgotten, and we took a solid eight-to-five step *backward* in progress.

"I know we've had a week off, you're sick of school already, and these are difficult sets- but really, guys! It's like you have all *shut down*. We need to wake up and start retaining information. If we don't, other bands are going to get ahead of us and we'll still be re-cleaning everything while everyone else learns body and horn moves and has the entire show learned." Mr. Padawan took a deep breath. He lifted the mic again after a moment of silence. "Take it back to the third." He clicked off the microphone and leaned forward from the top of the lift to watch.

The week ended on a high-but-ferociously-out-of-tune note that made everyone on campus cringe. The first trumpets decided to make up for the lack of volume from the rest of their section by putting everything into it and killing the note at "blastissimo" instead of fortissimo. Added to the varying intonation problems between the woodwinds and remaining brass sections, it was a malicious assault on the ears.

"Trumpets- John, don't play hero. Back down a little- the rest of your section should increase their volume. It's a team effort. Seconds and thirds, I need to hear you. Play out."

It was a relief that there were no more rehearsals until Monday. A three-day weekend was in order after the rude awakening that got us back into shape.

On Monday, we'll put our best foot forward and get our sets.

We can do this.

"Be prepared. On Monday, we're adding the fourth movement to our rehearsal."

Uh-oh…

Chapter 9: Burnout

From a distance, we could have been mistaken for a grazing herd of wild animals. Bumbling about in a state of complete confusion with no clear direction, no one would have guessed that we were putting the fourth movement of our show together…again.

"Did you guys forget everything we learned during band camp? You guys are a mess down there… reset to the last set of the third movement. Taking the first four sets, marching only, set by set. We'll work our way through the whole movement and then run it in chunks."

It was a rough rehearsal. After running circle drill, the rest of our time was spent repeating the chunks and refreshing our memory.

"There isn't enough time to relearn everything. We need to stay focused and retain what we learn. See you all tomorrow."

The next day brought a terror familiar to all students in marching bands everywhere: rehearsal without the metronome.

Weaning off the metronome was one of the scariest take-a-step-backward checkpoints in the marching season. With the metronome, which we began to rely on when learning, we were allowed to look around or face our dots and *listen* to stay in time. It was not how we were supposed to march, but it happened. Without the metronome, we were forced to rely on muscle memory and peripheral vision to gauge our own accuracy (by results) as we stared holes through the drum majors and *attempted* to stay in time.

With the met out, our music became more exposed; the blaring metronome echoing off the buildings often hides issues with our music.

We waited patiently. Mr. Padawan frowned at the brass section.

"Low brass and trumpets: I hear stick-outs." Stick-outs are one or two strong members in a section playing several dynamic levels louder than the whole rest of their section. Instead of sounding like a well-rounded wave of brass sound, it sounds less unified and less powerful overall.

Several runs later, he caught it again.

"Hey John, back off a little. The rest of the trumpets need to play out."

Not to be forgotten, the baritones- I mean, *a baritone*, got caught overpowering the rest of the band on a few measures of whole notes.

"Dominick, rein it in. You're overpowering the woodwinds."

He grinned and backed off, ignoring looks from the high winds.

It wasn't our fault we weren't as loud as the low brass. After all, the Collinsville low brass section has been legendary for its sound. (Not to say the Collinsville woodwinds weren't legendary, too- we could play runs that would scare the pants off of other woodwind sections!)

Meanwhile, the drummers drummed.

Our drummers made the rest of the world look sane. They're ridiculously funny and had a lot of hair, but could genuinely be mistaken for a couple of crazies.

Seriously, they had skill. For only having five members in the battery, the show still packed a punch. Adding them into the rehearsals with their parts, in addition to the pit, would keep the horn line from running away with the tempo during the crazy runs and the easy parts of the show.

Until we were ready, they marched and learned their drill without us.

"It's just easier to do without the rest of the band," said Marco, one of the sophomores.

James, one of the more lively drummers, agreed. "It's easy with just the five of us. There are fewer people to fix each run and everything moves a lot faster."

Time flew, and it was Friday- no after-school rehearsal.

During the week, the drums had added their drill to ours after working on a few spots. Most of the new kids and vacationers were successfully marching all the way through the third movement. Not bad, compared to how the week started.

There was only one week left until our first performance.

Chapter 10: Fallen

It's a bird! It's a plane! It's...*a baritone?*

It sailed through the air and landed a few feet beyond the fallen baritone player lying sprawled across the ground.

This was the second time a baritone player fell in the very first move of the show.

Prior to this, when running the first movement with the guard, Zach was the one to fall. The color guard had a circle set with flag-work later in the show, so they set up at the top of the show with their flags in that circle in the middle of the field. On the sixth step of the move, Zach tripped over a flag -instinctively hugging his baritone to his chest- and tumbled backward before quickly rolling to his feet, jumping right back into the run with the rest of us.

As soon as Kayla cut off our final note, the baritones exploded with laughter. The rest of the band just stared at the giggly section.

"Stop! Stop! Reset."

This time, however, Mr. Padawan stopped the run so no one could trample Anthony. Anthony picked himself off the ground and rubbed his head where it bumped the field. His marching baritone was lying where it landed, the bell bent outward and dented.

His pride survived the fall, and so did the baritone, which was fixed and returned in better –but not perfect- shape.

Marching band has risk for injury and risks for instruments, but usually it isn't this serious.

Anticipating the first real performance of the season at the end of the week, we dedicated a little time to aesthetics. From beginning to end, the show had to look polished and clean, as if we were really performing in a video or on Broadway- the show-off kind of performance.

Beginning the show was the first piece in the puzzle. The first downbeat sets the framework for the entire show, so a smooth way to begin without creating a tear between the timing of the pit and the main ensemble was in order.

Kayla and Nicole worked out a little system. Kayla subtly nodded to Nicole when the pit was ready to begin the show, and Kayla then jumped in to conduct.

The drum majors themselves were a power team, with magical timing-synchronization that baffled even the most musical of us to some degree. On the podiums, come rain or shine, they conducted through drastic tempo changes and confusing time signatures, almost always in unison, without missing a beat.

"Practice. That's all," they would say.

The leadership team amazed me. It was a prestigious role, we believed, to be a section leader, something most of us aspired to be eventually. Leadership meetings, which leaked only the tiniest snippets of details to everyone outside of them, were closed-door and after school, like a secret club or private council. Eventually I learned that it was mostly like a leadership course or a workshop, but it still retained that mysterious aura of importance and achievement. Most of the legendary players in recent years were all drum majors or student leaders, notably talented and authoritative people.

The primary function of Leadership was not to simply be the band director's police force, but to also lead by example and help us on the field. The drum majors couldn't offer individual help from the podium, so leaders had to take charge of correcting and rewarding when needed.

One of the other problems addressed over this time involved just that: unruly sections and respect issues.

It was restated and enforced that *only* leadership members should be responsible for correcting problems on the field- no general members should be telling one another (in theory) that they did this or that wrong and need to move here or there. As John put it, "There are too many chiefs. Too many people think they know everything. It's a problem."

We may all have had moments we thought we were right, but it was best to leave it to the leadership team and keep the peace.

Part 3: Spin

Chapter 11: Rush

Friday, September 2, 2011- The First Football Game

Our first performance was finally upon us.

Weeks of our hard work and dedication were about to be put to the test. For the first time, we would take the field on the actual football field (which, Padawan mentioned, actually *had* grass, but wasn't noticeably more level). And we were going to have an audience.

Even from the morning announcements in first hour mentioning the football game, I was nervous. I was actually dreading the final bell, wishing that Spanish class wouldn't end.

It worried all of us that we hadn't practiced even once on the actual football field. The lines would be a lot more accurate than on our practice field, the grass was torn up but still present, and the stadium lights would shine extremely bright in our faces.

It reeked of impending disaster. At least some of us thought so.

The final bell did ring after all, and everyone hurried their separate ways. Padawan asked the day before that we start our next after-school rehearsal early, and I still managed to be late because I had to get my uncooperative contact lenses in. Kayla was putting hers in when I walked upstairs, equally frustrated with hers. If I hadn't needed my peripheral vision so badly I would have skipped putting them in.

I was only a couple of minutes late to the rehearsal. The air was sweet and the sky clear, beautiful weather for the first Friday football game of the season. Our varsity Kahoks were about to face the Triad Knights, practicing for the game while we rehearsed on our patchy field.

For the first time, we got a taste of contest treatment: a moderate circle drill for warm-up and a variety of factory routines. Then, since we had the time, and it was only a home game, we hit the practice field and used a "chop-saving" air-first repetition, then a normal run-through of each section that actually needed the music rehearsed. *Chops* refers to the muscles in our mouths and lips that we have to tighten to play. They get really tired if we play for too long. It was always best not to overplay on contest or performance days.

The slight wind was almost chilly. The hot weather from band camp disappeared quickly after the end of August, and the slowly sinking sun sucked away most of the remaining warmth as it descended from the sky. By the time we would get to the bleachers at the football field, we would be comfortable in our stuffy black uniforms-uniforms we were about to wear for our very first marching performance (excluding parades).

At 5:00 on the dot, rehearsal ended and our section leaders passed out meal tickets. We carted our instruments and towels upstairs before dashing across the field toward the football field and the food stand where band parents were cooking brats, hamburgers, and nacho cheese. The drifting smoke from the grill made our stomachs rumble as we swarmed the table where a band parent was taking orders.

Hamburgers, nachos, or brats, a watery sports drink, and chips were our options for the *first* football game dinner of champions. Later on, after performing, band kids would storm the concessions stand once more and buy most of the remaining food after the game finishes.

The joke goes, band kids eat more after a

performance than the football team does…

We sat in the under-clothes of our uniforms (athletic shorts and t-shirts) on the speckled floor of the band hallway. We essentially had the run of the floor after-hours and dominated the main second floor hallway near the stairwell and bathrooms.

The bathrooms began to get busy as people competed for mirrors to put in contacts and apply eye-liner or pile hair on top of their heads to shove into the shakos, while others stood around inside the large bathrooms getting dressed into full uniform. Getting dressed into full uniform took several steps, beginning with athletic shorts and t-shirt and long black socks; then, the overalls that zipped in the front. Finally, there were the gloves, jacket, gauntlets, shoes, and shako to be put on.

There are many assumptions about band kids, some of which are not necessarily true, and others that are solid enough to bet on. One of these was that we were all weird because we helped dress one another. Nobody outside of band realized how difficult it is to zip the jackets by yourself or get shakos and gauntlets on straight. The same went for getting out of uniform after performances-choruses of "unzip me, please!" traveled around the band room.

Also, it was mostly the section leaders who roamed the room policing uniforms. Most commonly a flute or clarinet player walked up to another member, shoved their instrument into one hand and water into the other of the trapped band kid, and proceeded to straighten shakos, tighten or flip backward gauntlets, zip jackets, or even tie shoes. (I think this was because we tended to be the nit-picky members of the ensemble, though it was not always the case.) The same goes for concerts. For some reason, half of the guys could never get their bowties on straight…

"*Mom!* Fix my gauntlets- they're too loose!" Liz ran up to me, invoking my nickname. I tightened the gauntlets before turning around to help zip up a freshman saxophone player and retrieve my flute.

The band room was flooded with moving black and purple uniforms covering all but the faces of students peeping out from beneath the shakos. Surrounding us, the floor was littered with empty uniform bags laying near lockers in haphazard, slippery piles.

Molly, Kayla, and Staci all reappeared in our midst, clapping their hands and waving to get our attention. It was nearly time to go. They instructed us to go outside to the concrete area near the practice field and the sidewalk leading to the football field and wait in the official parade block: flutes in the first line, then clarinet rows (five people to a row), saxophones, mellophones, trumpets, baritones, tubas, and the drums. Pit members were loading their equipment onto the tractor-trailer for drop-off on the flat tracks surrounding the field.

We bumbled out of the band room's double doors, down the dust white stairwell, and out the doors. Rob, the percussion assistant, lurked near the drums and listened as they practiced their parts in the show.

The guard followed shortly after, sporting makeup masks that highlighted their eyes with amber and ruby flames flickering toward their cheekbones. The guard was down a few members from the beginning of the season due to a minor car accident and an injury, but with the incredible dances and usage of eye-catching golden swing-flags (flags with a shorter handle and wider flag that are used in pairs), the guard made a powerful, intricately audience-engaging presence on the field. We made the song, but they gave the music a body. It took their graceful dancing to help convey emotions and feelings and to give the band a more polished look.

Once outside, we formed our block and played quietly to ourselves the parts that we worried about the most. Earlier in the week, Padawan made his executive decision that movement four wasn't quite clean enough to perform at this game. Instead, we would play movements one through three on the move and movement four in the arch set at the end of movement three. I was relieved, because it seemed that each time I spun around from the double circle set into the thirty-two-count hold in movement four, I was either out of my line too far forward or off-center- which was bad, because I was in the very front on the right side of the field. At least I only had three movements to worry about messing up for the evening.

The tubas bellowed whole notes, beginning our tuning sequence. Then, it was time to go.

Like a line of proud tin soldiers we marched silently in a single-file line, following the drum majors toward the football field. Winding along the sidewalk with instruments in trail position (the way we carry instruments on, off, or toward a performance area, a comfortable and uniform position that varies in each section), our shadows stretched out to the grass in the dim light spilling over the vocational wing of the school from the stadium lights on the other side, clutching at the practice field we were leaving as if to say, "No! We're not ready yet!" We dragged along these phantoms as we left the safety of our territory and entered unfamiliar grounds. Perhaps this was not so moving an experience to the veterans of the band, but the journey from our practice field to the football field was a monumental one for the first-year members.

Bubbly stadium-noises rolled across the field and bounced off of the wooded hills on our right, reaching us suddenly as we trooped past the maintenance shed and the old botany class greenhouse with dusty green glass windows presently devoid of plant life. Bright and dull hues blended together in the crowd that milled about in the stands, an evening rainbow beneath the stadium lights with purple splotches of spectators representing our home team, the Collinsville Kahoks, and a large purple and white stripe in the reserved student-section. It wasn't a large crowd, but the stands were remarkably full for the first game of the season. (At a full-house game like the Homecoming Game, there isn't enough seating in the bleachers and people stand all around the short chain link fence that surrounds the track and field to watch the game.)

My knees shook a little as we filed onto the track near the end zone without the scoreboard. A freshman in the middle of the line tripped over a dip in the concrete in his nervousness.

Once on the track, we resumed standard parade block formation. Band parents arrived toting boxes full of our glossy black feather plumes, which they began to attach to our shakos. As we waited for pluming and the tuning exercise, I stared at the crowd.

The bleachers seemed gigantic to me. Suddenly I felt dizzy and my heart attempted to jump out of my chest.

"Molly! I'm scared! I can't do this!"

It wasn't me who spoke. It was a freshman whose eyes seemed about to pop out and was practically dancing in spot as if her feet were on hot coals.

Molly and Staci, who had heard the exclamation and came over to reassure the freshman, smiled.

"Don't worry. Everyone feels like this the first time. I'm nervous too. Just watch Kayla, Molly, or me." Staci said.

Molly straightened the frightened girl's shako, fluffed the plume, and patted her shoulder. "You'll do fine. You've got the rest of the band- all of your friends- on the field with you. Just trust them like they trust you."

We tuned again, straightened out lines, and prepared to step out as a snare drum began a brisk roll-off sequence. *Brrrump-brum! Brrrump-brum! Bruuhduhduhduh-bruhduhduhduh-dumdum!* Push, one. The trumpets attacked their triumphant opening notes of our parade tune, and we began to march down the curve of the track, past the food stand where many of our parents were working to fundraise for the band.

The cheerleading squad, which was warming up and waving pom-poms at the gathering audience, moved aside to give us space. We halted where they had been, and turned to face the audience in the bleachers.

Bum-bum. Bum-bum.

It seemed like I had barely blinked when we were called to attention as Kayla brought her hands up and gave the downbeat for the National Anthem. Then Molly and Staci directed us for our fight songs.

We waited until the first kickoff to make our way back to our tiny, lone set of bleachers to the right side of the field (home side perspective). Shakos, gauntlets, jackets, and even gloves came off while we rested, instruments sitting in the rows in front of us out of the way. The guard was seated up to the right, near trumpets and low brass, whereas flutes and clarinets were in the front left next to Mr. Padawan, Alyssa, Rob, and the other techs who attended the game.

There we sat, some of us more nervous than others, for the whole first period and about three game minutes of the second, until we were instructed to put on everything but our shakos and walk over to the end zone where we had assembled at earlier.

Bum-bum. Bum-bum.

My pulse quickened.

Nerves kicked in viciously.

It was time to perform.

We stood cramped together beneath the field goal at the end zone, in parade block, when the whistle blew to signal the start of half time. *Only twenty minutes until the athletes return to the field, after we perform our show for the first time of the season.*

Twenty minutes until my personal performing nightmare would be over.

"...Please welcome the Collinsville Marching Kahoks to the field!"

That was our cue. Weston began a steady drum cadence to march to as we marched clear across the field to the fifty-yard line. I kept my eyes glued on Padawan, who was walking backward with us while facing us and guiding us. We barely noticed the crowd cheer wildly as we began our procession.

"Deep breaths, guys. Take deep breaths." He whispered. "Okay, go find your spots while Molly, Kayla, and Staci do their thing."

I was at the very front, in the center of the field. I turned right to count the yard lines and find my spot, glancing over to look at the emptiness of the front half of the field, highlighted a vivid green-yellow under the stadium lights. I peeled my eyes away and made the long, twenty-yard walk to my yard line, the thirty.

Bum-bum. Bum-bum. Bum-bum.

I was the last to take a seat of my little group of four, aside from Molly, who took her spot behind me to the left. Time seemed to freeze as Molly and Staci joined us after performing their salute and Kayla made her way to the top of the tallest podium.

It was customary for drum majors to make a salute to the crowd (or the judges, at competition) before performing. Not only does it show the honor of this role, but it also looks really, really cool. Marching bands *love* to look cool.

Kayla stood motionless for a moment atop the podium. Finally, she lifted her hands. I took one last deep breath, closing my eyes and sucking in a lung-full of air. I opened my eyes when the bass drum attacked the very first beat of the show.

The applause died away long after we left the field.

Sweating like perspiring drinking glasses with frosted sides, we managed to strip to half-uniform faster than ever before. Gloves, gauntlets, shakos, and jackets flew off. I blinked as the light hit me in the eyes, which had been shielded by my shako, and readjusted to the brightness.

On the field, everything ceased to make sense except dots and music. There was no crowd, no bats fluttering between stadium lights above, no time except the tempo, no air except that in our horns, until the final chord when our eyes began to glaze and Kayla cut us off. At that moment, time restarted.

We breathed, thought, whispered, saw and heard, the magic tucked away safely once more until the next performance, hiding in our horns and the tight spaces in the hollow parts of our shakos. Some of us trembled with leftover excitement, shell-shocked and relieved all at once.

Something golden truly *had* flown between members on the field, near the beginning of the show. However, *that* wasn't the magic. It was mellophone leader Jordan Olive's mouthpiece that flew over his shoulder when he snapped his horn up into playing position quickly. (Later on, a coach found it and handed it to Padawan, who in turn gave it back to Jordan.)

Collinsville lost to Triad, but the game was riveting and the action continuous. The band sat in its bleachers for the rest of the fourth quarter after running around and eating during the third, yelling, talking, laughing, and even dancing to cell phone music in the seats. The game finished, and we played the fight song one final time; then, silent but for the beat of a drum, we marched back the way we came, proud tin soldiers trooping back to our little tin box for the night, our little tin horns drooping from tired but proud arms.

That night, in the presence of all our peers and the parents of Collinsville, we learned that we could do all we sought to do with courage, faith in ourselves and the drum majors, and a lot of practice.

We had come so far…

…And yet, we had a *long* way to go.

Chapter 12: Rooster Booster

Saturday, September 3, 2011- Fairview Heights Wing Festival

The smells wafting through the mid-morning air were making my stomach rumble and my mouth water. Several of us gazed at nearby food vendors, pining for the delicious food they were slaving over at their grills.

Why oh why did the gig have to be at the Fairview Heights Wing Festival at ten in the morning?

Anyone who has ever woken up forty-five minutes late and had to get up and go with only a puny granola bar in his or her stomach will understand the agony. *Especially* because a cook-off competition was beginning, and about twenty different saliva-triggering flavors filled each breath of air we took for the twenty-five minutes we warmed up, tuned, and waited to perform.

At 8:15 a.m. we had assembled at the high school. We loaded our gear onto the buses and the truck designated for the percussion's pit equipment. I clearly remember the way many of the female guard and band members looked when they walked into the school: tired and half-savage. Moments later, they emerged from the bathroom looking distinctly more civilized. Many had simply rolled out of bed and gone to school.

"I'm tired," was heard about fifty times from different people I talked to. The previous night's football game kept us busy until after ten. This was the life of the marching band student: work hard during the week (or play, if you consider it that!), perform at a long and cold (or hot) football game on Friday night, and compete on Saturday. This is where the phrase "band is like family" is proven: you spent more hours a day with them; ate more meals with them; took more trips with them; tagged them on social networks as sisters, brothers, aunts and uncles; and squabble and caused mischief like a family. However, they would not record your performance for you as your real family would, bring you flowers like your parents might, bring you food money or a blanket for sitting in the bleachers, nor even gush about your talent to other adults; they were on the field with you, and might have laughed if you asked them for any of these things. We appreciated our band family, but nothing could replace our own families- especially when they embarrass us with loving and weird shout-outs at competitions right before we perform.

We arrived half-awake, excited for our first gig. Mr. Padawan told us what an excellent opportunity it was for us, both to raise funds and to send the message to other bands that this year, Collinsville was *serious*. (The band grapevine was high-speed; word travelled like wildfire between directors and programs.)

The rest of the weekend would be ours to spend; this morning was for the band-family.

Standing on the ground in an arch in front of a stage set up for later performers, we waited for our pit to roll into place. Frequently we fidgeted and pushed our shakos down further on our heads to shade our eyes from the high sun above. Molly, Kayla, and Staci exchanged looks before stepping forward to begin.

Mr. Padawan motioned for them to wait. Moments later, a voice over a loudspeaker announced the official start of the Fairview Heights Wing Festival.

"Please welcome the Collinsville High School

Marching Band, performing the National Anthem, American Finale, and *Solaris: Sun Rise, Sun Culture, Rays of the Sun, The Cycle Ends,* and *Apocalyptic*."

Old Glory fluttered gracefully nearby at the front of a building as we played the National Anthem. When we began to play our marching show in place without any of our body moves, it was more difficult to tell where we came in, and a saxophone brought the band in two measures early. Luckily, the pit caught on and cut out two measures to adjust their part to ours: crisis averted.

After that little mishap, everything went beautifully. The guard performed swirling flag spins and tossed their rifles like spinning white blades, slicing invisible holes through the thick cloud of heat that engulfed us. The drum line pounded each downbeat like a mighty cannon firing a salute. Weaving between the two distinct melodies, the pit sang a ritualistic song with the delicate touches of the marimba and the smashing abruptness of the bass drum.

The sun shone down brightly. The moment our performance ended, we blinked as the dust cleared and turned slowly to march away in organized lines back to the buses.

The feelings that left with us from the performance were a little different from after our football game. Playing the show together for a live performance had a thrill of its own, but it just didn't feel the same to play it standing still. The show, with its intricate rhythm and spiraling, smashing ending, felt so intense to play or listen to that it felt strange to imagine rituals, dances, and the world crumbling while standing still. This piece was made for movement, fit only for the field because it *belonged* there;

without the movement, there wasn't the thrill and magic that we craved.

We learned our true priorities: it wasn't about the crowd, the attention, or the competition (although we did love to compete).

We performed because together we became something else, something that nothing could take down, something that loss or hardships could not defeat. As a group, making our magic on the field, we moved and breathed as one mighty entity. When we acted as a team, nothing could break us.

I didn't know how true this was until much, much later, nor could I imagine how much a marching band could take without breaking.

Chapter 13: We Must Never Forget

Friday, September 9, 2011

Our evening began just as our morning began: in silence and in memories.

The principal of Collinsville High School evoked our faint memories of the tragic events of September 11, 2001 during the morning announcements with a solemn tribute of words to the memory of those killed in the attacks. After a moment of silence, he continued with the usual morning announcements. It seemed that old wounds were still very fresh and real for the nation, especially on the tenth anniversary of the attacks.

In the cooled, less-muggy evening air, we suppressed the urge to fidget, only daring to blink or twitch our fingers while standing in our statue-like poses at attention, with our instruments held in front and silently rehearsing rhythms. The announcer, somewhere obscured from my view by the bleachers, gave a long, mournful introduction to the game. Dignified, we stood stock-still until Kayla was cued to direct *The Star Spangled Banner*.

The misting rain ceased, leaving our metal band bleachers uncomfortably cold and wet. Earlier, when we rehearsed on the practice field, sheets of rain soaked us for ten solid minutes. Afterward, it was a continuous mist until we shuffled over to get our food at the concession stand. Despite the rain, since it hadn't really soaked the field, we would perform our show as usual, including our opening sit-down body moves. We would just have to deal with the wet seats of our uniforms quietly.

The bleachers weren't exceptionally full, but filled enough to raise a decent applause as we shuffled along the track to our seats and peeled off gloves and shakos.

The most awkward thing about marching in parades or on the field was having a wobbly, fluffy plume bobbing around on the top of one's shako that feels the equivalent of having a large bird perched on it. Unless the head was constantly held relatively level (assuming the plume hasn't been bent when inserted into the shako), there is uncertainty about the appearance and discomfort due to those bird feathers. It was a dead giveaway to judges concerning bad posture if the plume was at an angle instead of straight up.

"Let's go Kahoks!" *Clap, clap, clap-clap-clap.*

"Let's go defense!"

"Let's go offense!"

For as hot as the days were in Collinsville in early September, the nights got rather cool, even without rain. Up in the bleachers, band kids sat comfortably in the uniform jackets or comfortable matching band jackets ordered earlier in the year. Some of the guard members looked a little cold in their one-sleeve outfits. At least nobody would be cold after the performance.

The first quarter ended. Time to go warm up at the end zone.

In a long, quick procession we paraded one by one to the end zone. The grill from the concession stands was located dreadfully close; with every shift in the weak breeze, the smells of sizzling burgers and juicy hot dogs drifted over, making our stomachs rumble.

The crowd cheered as a player threw a long pass. Neither Collinsville nor Alton seemed to have a definite lead. Most of the plays were lasting a bit longer that usual, which meant less time for us to get ready.

I saw many changes from the first game the previous week. There was no threat of failure or dread of defeat. We knew our stuff, had performed *Solaris* once already, and no longer doubted ourselves. We were confident that the second game performance would run just as the first: smoothly. The seasoned members were collected and confident.

I almost considered looking over my shoulder to check if Jordan had put tape on his mouthpiece so it wouldn't fly off again.

Tap. Tap. Rat-tat-tat.

The lone beats of a snare announced our presence on the field and guided our feet. The crowd, though mildly noisy, was non-existent on the field. The bleachers full of color became just objects- no audience, no judgment. It was incredibly loud and incredibly quiet all at once on the field.

There was no place so open and scary as the football field under the stadium lights when it was time to begin a half-time marching show.

Something didn't feel right about my shoes- they felt like giant clown shoes. It felt like I was going to trip if I took another step. *Well, there's nothing I can do about it until after the performance.*

What happened next was nearly a disaster only averted because of my nerves. In the "Green Lantern" move straight across the field, when I had to take large steps backward, the heel of my shoe caught the grass and I almost fell. Luckily, since the move made me nervous anyway, I was prepared enough and caught myself in time for the next move. (Later on I found out that my shoes were two and a half sizes too big!)

On the sidelines, Kaitlynn Brown was in her element. Surrounded by the pounding drums and flashing cameras, her heart began to pound. The excitement was almost too much to handle. Only when the music stopped could she slow her pulse and catch her breath.

"I've got this down."

This was the general feeling of the band after our performance.

Freshman Rachel Smith, a clarinet player, was all smiles when we walked off the field. "The crowd doesn't matter. I'm proud because I love band and I don't care what anyone says otherwise."

Courtney Griffith, the mellow junior mellophone player, was just relieved it was over and her nerves could calm down.

After the game, per usual, we trooped back to the commons area in a single line and twisted into a tight spiral around Mr. Padawan for comments and dismissal. After he congratulated us on a good performance, he reminded us that next week there was no football game, although we did have the Edwardsville competition –a new one this year- and the Italian Festival after the competition.

Our excitement lasted from that moment through all of the next week. Competitions mean performing, hanging out with friends, and food; *most importantly,* food. Besides, it was exciting to watch our competitors and compare shows.

After all, we were told repeatedly that we were doing great and stood a chance of winning

We had yet to find out if this was true.

Chapter 14: Sending a Message

Saturday, September 17, 2011- Edwardsville Ambush Classic Marching Competition

Early in the morning, when we walked through the double doors of the band room covered with fliers, the noise of the door creaking open and swinging shut cracked the silence in half.

In lieu of a football game last night, many of us stayed up even later doing other things like homework and playing game consoles or watching movies. The poor sleeping plans don't affect us much; we manage to catch some sleep practically anywhere.

Band members were sprawled across the floor on their backs, slumped against band lockers, and sleeping with instrument cases as pillows. Aside from those sleeping, others whispered quietly or wore serious expressions while sifting through drawstring bags and messy lockers, searching for gloves or stray bobby pins.

It was quiet because every member was nervous. It was a new competition, and the first of the season. Adding to the pressure was the fact that in order to compete and make it back with enough time to march in the annual Italian Festival Parade, we were scheduled specially (and kindly, by the organizers of the competition) to perform roughly three hours before our assigned time, before the smaller bands and our rivals in our class.

We didn't have long to relax; after our short warm-up and rehearsal outside on the concrete near the dewy practice field, it was time to help the pit load their marimbas and other sideline equipment onto the truck. The members of the pit really did have the most equipment to keep track of: instruments, cords, bags, microphones, tarps, and the occasional tambourine. With the extra help, loading took less than half an hour.

We gathered our instruments and double-checked our uniforms, then loaded the buses. The sky looked as if a storm was brewing right over our heads.

One of the wacky traditions some members practice involved competition bracelets. At the beginning of the season, from the first competition, bracelets were worn every day, all the time, and left on until they fell off. The more practical version was wearing all of the bracelets collected over the season(s) at once only on competition days. Edwardsville's neon orange bands would make nice additions to the collections on display.

About seventy band kids and staff members squished into the two yellow school buses. The smell of valve oil and lemons drifted through the stale bus air.

Brass and woodwinds had their own pre-contest traditions. One designated brass member brought a plastic bag full of lemon wedges. On the ride to the contest, the brass sucked on the lemons to pucker their embouchures (mouth shape for playing any particular instrument; in this case, shaping to the round mouth pieces the brass use). Apparently this helped them hit high notes on the field that required tight embouchure.

The woodwinds' tradition was the opposite: sweet. One designated senior brought a bag of sugar cubes and each person got one cube. The older members of band claimed that it helped their playing ability on the field, but I'm sure the sugar rush was the primary benefit behind that tradition.

Participating in these events took our minds off the

pressures of competition for a little while.

The wheels on the bus go round and round...

Ok, we never really sang that song. Band kids, if they were actually going to sing (and be forewarned, *some* love music of both kinds but chose band because they couldn't sing well enough for choir!), sang the popular tunes at the time or Christmas tunes when approaching the holiday season. I've heard *Journey* songs so many times I could toss my sugar cube…

"Whoa! Look at their field!"

I knew we had arrived before I leaned over to look up over the seats at the object of everyone's present attention. Through the wide glass window I saw vast expanses of green. Green, plush grassy soccer fields flanked us parallel to a turf stadium with tall, gleaming metal bleachers. The absence of the sun brought a distinct chill to the mild air- maybe it was just nerves.

The bus pulled into a spot next to the guard and percussion bus.

Silently, like a line of ants streaming out of an anthill, we climbed out of the bus, formed two straight lines behind John Bailey and me (brass and woodwind lines), and followed the drum majors and Mr. Padawan across a crowded parking lot. Another high school band with thirty members was warming up.

They stared as we walked by. It made the nervous feelings return- the same throat-clenching fear as the night of the first football game, with the exact eerie silence and hole in the pit of my stomach that cooled my muscles and made my heart begin to pound.

It was only the walk to the farthest soccer field for

a short warm-up, but it was terrifying. (I was, most certainly, a pansy.)

The grass of the soccer field was thick. No matter how we tried to adjust when pushing off, our traveling feet managed to catch on the grass and trip us up during our condensed, rapid version of factory.

When we returned to our places in the circle by our shakos to be plumed, some volunteer band moms frantically wiped the tops of our shoes with baby wipes to clean off the wet grass clippings clinging to them.

Our frustration over the grass and the early time in the morning caught Mr. Padawan's attention.

"Guys- I can tell you're nervous. *Don't be*. You've had your music and known it since July. You've got this."

Fidgeting, we pretended we were collected and calm. Some truly were calm; I could tell by looking at members like my brother, the confident veteran- but most of us couldn't hide it well enough to make the case for confidence.

Last night, my brother told me a horrible tale about the perils of slippery turf. By now, I was imagining the equivalent of a wet kitchen floor or a slick water slide and all the painful or embarrassing ways I could fall and ruin the show.

"Pay attention." Mr. Padawan paused. "Right now, you guys are *everywhere*. It's loud, it's misting, and it's early in the morning, I know. This is important."

Padawan turned as he talked, meeting our eyes, addressing us as if talking to each person individually.

"Collinsville is going on first. The judges haven't heard a single note yet. It's tough, because we have to play hours before our class because of the parade." He glanced up with a comical annoyed look on his face, and looked back at us. "It's tough because the other guys in our group will be fresh in their minds when they make the decision. Don't make it about them, and what they've got going for them. We're here to send a message.

"Think about the way you rehearse. It's the same music you've practiced over and over again, the same moves, the same drill. We warm up the same way, attack the same way each time, and move together. *They* don't do the things we do. They don't breathe the same, attack the same, or play with the volume you do. Just play like you do in rehearsal. It's not about a rough performance or little mistakes or even a *fantastic* performance. *It's about who we are.*"

A band student from Edwardsville arrived to guide us to the field.

It was show-time.

"Don't worry, guys. Just do your best."

While we trekked to the stadium, on a path that led us through a tunnel under the road , the clouds stopped spitting water onto us. The sun remained absent for our dignified march toward our first performance.

When we arrived at the outer gate of the field, an Edwardsville High School student belted out the final notes of *The Star-Spangled Banner* and the audience sat back down. After the applause died, we moved quietly inside the stadium gates. A man with a badge and a walkie-talkie in a bright yellow windbreaker waved us through the gates.

The announcer read off the names of the judges. It seemed like everything was unusually slow while we anticipated performing.

"Once you find your spot, take a few deep breaths. Relax. Don't forget to watch the drum majors," Padawan whispered back to us.

"Collinsville High School Marching Band, you may take the field!"

Exactly as we had at the last two football games, we followed Padawan and the drum majors all the way to the fifty yard line, then split for our spots.

I followed Katelyn and Rachel nervously to our formation and carefully sat down, crossing my legs. The wet turf soaked my gloves and dampened the seat and legs of my uniform.

Kayla, Molly, and Staci saluted the judges, then took their places on the field and on top of the podium. As Molly and Staci made their way back to the woodwind formations, they cracked grins and fist-bumped. Kayla removed her shako, shook free her braided hair, smiled, then raised her hands to conduct.

For a moment, our eyes shifted to Nicole, a red-headed percussionist in the pit. When Kayla gives the signal (a slight movement of her hand), Nicole drops the beat and begins the whole show.

Nicole held both mallets loosely in her hands. The moment Kayla gave the signal she tightened her grip, dipped her mallets once for tempo, and hammered the opening beats into the drum.

The color guard, sitting on their legs in a kneeling position, rolled sideways, arched their backs, leapt from the ground and spun away. We began our dance, instantly catching the full attention of the crowd.

The trumpets formed their line parallel to that of the woodwinds reaching for the front; then, joining for the hold in lines across the field, the low brass took over and drove our feet with booming short notes.

Breathe, two. Breathe, two. Step out, breathe.

There was just something about the teamwork on the field that took the terror out of marching. Even at this performance, with little nervous blunders and accidentally missed notes, knowing that the team was on the field with you minimized the mental trauma from mistakes and padded confidence with a soft layer of protection. The band moved on regardless of little mishaps like almost going the wrong direction after a hold. *It happens to everyone, right?*

Eons later, and in no time at all at the same time, we froze at the final note of the fourth movement. In the moment- while marching- nerves disappear and eventually come crashing back once the performance was done. Waiting those long seconds for Kayla to release us was as stressful, if not more, than the actual duration of the performance.

The crowd had a good laugh when we began to exit the field to the right and had to turn around to exit the proper way.

Mr. Padawan and the drum majors were smiling.

It was not a bad performance- not bad at all.

Within fifteen minutes we were back on the buses. We would have to wait a few hours for the rest of our class to compete before we could hear about our placement.

Kayla stepped onto the bus, yelled, "*Hey, guys!*" to get our attention, and took attendance to make sure everyone was accounted for.

"John." Check.

"Chris." Check.

"Abby."

"Phil." And so on.

After every name had been checked, or so Kayla thought, Phil Collins, a lively freshman baritone player, stood up. "You forgot to call someone."

"Who?" Kayla frowned, squinting at her sheet.

"You forgot *sexy*." Everyone sandwiched in the crowded bus seats rippled with laughter. Phil sat back down, smirking.

"Oh." Kayla laughed and smiled. "Is sexy here?"

"PRESENT!" we screamed.

Our other commitment for the day, the annual Italian Festival, was a local tradition and fundraiser for buildings with ample parking space downtown. The festival recognized the Italian heritage of Collinsville and showcased local talent, services, and specialty cooking of recipes dusted off for the occasion.

The usual circuit for parades was a simple square route stretching a handful of blocks in the center of Collinsville that passed the local library and circled back to the funeral home parking lot that we warmed up in. It was not a difficult route, although it was normally hot and the crowd always bulged off the designated sidewalk area toward the lane for parade traffic. (In a past parade, when the crowd got way too far into the street, someone was struck and knocked out accidentally by a flag pole from one of the guard girls.) In short, the band was a little tired by the time we were dropped off at our parking lot to warm up and could have done well with a nap in between.

Within the hour it took to warm up, the humidity spiked and thick, boiling thunderclouds crept toward the patch of sky above us. The crowd held its attendance and the ominous clouds accumulating above kept quiet for a short time.

Just as for the competition, we warmed up in a circle drill form, practicing in the grass by the funeral home parking lot. Across the street the middle school band warmed up and milled around, waving to us or yelling across the road. Considering our long morning and current drained energy levels, Mr. Padawan directed us to take off the uniform jackets and focused on air-only exercises for the first half of the time we waited. (The Collinsville High School marching band was near the middle-end of the parade, and the middle school was one of the very last in the lineup. We had a pretty long wait, considering it was a local festival parade.)

Eventually the little troop of Girl Scouts moved from our side street onto the main road for the parade. We took their place in a neat parade block and stood waiting. Shuffling our feet and turning to talk with neighbors, fifteen more minutes passed. (The Italian Festival parade features many pageant toddlers, politicians, and banks advertisements, which stretches the parade in length and time.)

Finally! It was time to step off. Others around me groaned as they put shakos back on and inched back into their correct spots.

Molly walked among us, making sure our ears were tucked under the edge of the shakos and that they sat firmly wedged onto our heads.

"Alright, shakos on. Get ready."

Staci was standing directly in front of me. Drum majors walked forward when we were marching at carry and not playing during a parade, until a drum gave a loud roll-off. Then, in the four counts before the beginning of our parade tune, they spun around to face us and marched backwards while directing. They were dependent upon some basic eye and facial communications to know whether or not there was something they could not see in their path that they must avoid, or if the groups ahead had stopped and stanched the flow of parade floats through the streets.

"Ready?" Padawan stood off to our left. "I'll give you eight counts, then come in marking time with a drum cadence. Set to carry." (Carry was how we held for parades; standby was just not playing while marching. Some bands used other terms for these positions.)

"One…two… One, two three, mark! Left, left…"

The very first move of the parade for us was a "left gate" or left turn. To turn neatly in parades, we mimicked a hinged gate. The "inside" member close to the curb we are turning towards took little steps, and the "outside" marcher took large steps, maintaining a neat line.

There are three ways to carry instruments in a parade for brass and woodwind performers: playing position, carry, and trail. Carry is holding the instrument out in front ready to bring to playing position and trail is holding the instrument in a comfortable way to give arm muscles a rest from holding an instrument up (this is especially appreciated by the mellophones and baritones) during drum cadences and between reps of the parade tune.

Ahead of us was a gaudy float draped in white crepe paper with balloons. Standing on it was a couple being married throughout the parade. This was definitely a first; for all the years we had attended or marched in the Italian Fest Parade, I cannot remember any parade weddings. The couple looked dreadfully hot in their formal attire, exposed to the sun without anything to shade them, not even a canopy. The bridesmaids and groomsmen followed the float on the ground.

We began our march. Every block or two we performed our music, carefully avoiding crushed candies and sticky globs of gum littering the pavement. The color guard spun with their flags and smiled gracefully ahead of us. Alyssa, Rob, and Mr. Padawan, as well as several band parents in matching purple polos, walked alongside us.

The crowd cheered for us as we passed. We dutifully ignored flashing cameras and waving friends to the best of our abilities, determined to look professional. At each corner we focused on turning in straight, impressive lines. It was important, after all, to look our best; we had several generations of marchers (past and future) watching.

It seemed like an eternity until we marched the final block back to our parking lot. Our pants legs and gloves were damp with sweat, and we were thoroughly exhausted.

Though not as exhilarating or exciting as full marching competitions, parades felt good. When half the city was standing at the sides of the road watching and clapping for you, it felt wonderful. Parades were nothing to sweat about, unless it was hot and extremely humid.

At the end of the parade, Padawan announced our placement at the competition after calling the parents that stayed for the competition.

Collinsville took third place for the bronze prize at the Edwardsville competition.

"For going on *three hours early*, that is great!" Padawan crowed. We were filled with pride and determination by our ranking at the competition.

"You've sent a message that Collinsville is *serious* this year. We've got a shot at first prize at GSL."

"Are you ready to rise to the challenge?"

Chapter 15: Great Things to Come

September 19-23, 2011

Aside from our progress on the field, other momentous events shook our band. With our bronze prize at Edwardsville and further upcoming rehearsals, we were travelling a course destined to end somewhere great.

The entire band learned the body for the fourth movement hold. It was a rippling, two-count staggered drop-and-kneel move that directed every instrument toward the flag "sun" in the middle of the ensemble.

The low brass, during that same rainy indoor-rehearsal, learned their "hops" for the transition from the first movement into the second. To their set of driving eighth note beats on counts one and three for several measures, the baritones literally jumped from foot to foot and switched leg positions on the beat. The concentration and determination on their faces was apparent as they struggled to attack each note while jumping without splitting each note.

From our placement at the Edwardsville *Tiger Ambush Classic Marching Competition*, we found out that the Collinsville marching band would be, for sure, in the smallest category at GSL, the blue category. This meant we would be competing with bands like Parkway West and Marquette High School. In fact, despite being in the smallest group, our competition wouldn't be all tiny schools with fewer than thirty marchers. The blue division has had some tough champions, and never before had Collinsville taken a first place award in any division at that competition.

On Friday, September 23, our third football game was rained out for the band. We performed everything in a double-arc at the front of the field to avoid damaging the soggy sod or potential injuries from slipping while marching. Despite it being dreary and cold, we received a grand applause from our audience.

The most exciting news of the season came from one school board meeting. The annual band trip proposed for a week in Disney World was approved, which made the students extra-hyper and excitable. Having most of a week to run around with friends in Florida sounded like a great idea, and after the success from fundraising with discount concert cards, was within the band's means.

So we sat waiting for the last incredible bit of news one day in class, half asleep or fidgeting energetically after learning about Disney, already planning in our heads how much fun we would have. Our jaws dropped, however, when Mr. Padawan confirmed a rumor.

Rumor had it that someone proposed fixing our football field that was costing many thousands of dollars a year to fix and re-sod twice a year by replacing it with a turf field. Turf is the synthetic grass used in major league football stadiums like the Edward Jones Dome in St. Louis. Instead of needing redone every year like normal grass, turf lasts for ten or more years with one large initial cost.

We had all heard whispers of hope for our program, and then Padawan confirmed it. The tentative budget was approved; the measure was going to a vote. Only positive things could come from the installation of the turf: fewer injuries, less cost over the years, and the potential to hold competitions at the school in the future.

The future looked extremely bright for us, as bright as the sun.

Chapter 16: Redemption

Saturday, September 24, 2011, Lafayette Marching Competition

The thick grass crushed softly beneath our feet as we trailed behind Padawan like black and white puppies in half-uniform, carrying our jackets and shakos tucked under our arms. We bumbled through the grass across the hilly landscaping surrounding the parking lot at Lafayette High School toward the warm-up field.

Lafayette was one of the most enjoyable competitions to go to (second only to McKendree so far) and watch other bands after performing. The secret was the mix of yummy food, bleachers (or hills) to sit on with the band, and a friendly atmosphere combined with great weather. So far, the day was not disappointing. September flew by with all the rehearsals and competitions, taking with it the notoriously high temperatures of summer and ushering in the cool, crisp winds and biting frost of October. As of 11:45 a.m. when we began to warm up, the temperature was mild, and brisk winds poked through the seams of the uniforms. My friends and I looked forward to relaxing on the bleachers with warm blankets to watch other bands compete after our performance.

Nearby, a girl clad in a gray leotard with black and red accents practiced running and leaping into the arms of a boy in a tuxedo (without the jacket) for their show. Later I learned that this was for their show titled *Heartbeat*, which became one of our favorite shows to watch later on.

First, in the grass, we set up our parade block formation to practice factory. We used our techniques and our complaining muscles to push through the rigid patches of grass. The first time through the side-to-side exercise we were not paying attention and had to re-do the exercise. It was crucial to get our heads in the game and *stay there*.

It wasn't that we were not trying. Even good bands have bad mornings, and this was certainly one of them for us.

We weren't in gear. Maybe it was the nature of the competition: Lafayette selects the top ten bands of the day based upon score (regardless of size) to make finals in which they would compete later on for final placement. Walking into *any* performance expecting defeat ultimately factors into how a team performs. Or, maybe we were nervous again. The color guard still had the old parade uniforms to use while waiting for the new show outfits to arrive, and we were still adding body moves to the show. From where we stood we could see the props and tarps from other bands' shows; we were alone on the field, and we had no props to use as a visual aid or a crutch. We had only our music and our bodies to tell our story.

We would have to shine or burn out on our own power.

The circle warm-up on the asphalt parking lot went much better. Perhaps we stood a chance after all.

A young woman with a badge on a lanyard came to fetch us and take us to the end-zone where the band before us was performing.

It was time to find out.

The strangest transition in marching band was that for performance: we got quiet, got into uniforms, and got serious. And sometimes, we got lucky.

Consciously, we were enthusiastic and confident as we waited on the far sideline while another group finished their show and cleared the field. Mr. Padawan stood with us, waiting to release us onto the stubby grass field for our turn. Meanwhile, an announcer read off air-grams.

"To Collinsville: Mellophones, you left a *SHOE* on the sideline! Go band!" The humorous shout-out, involving the funny nickname of Ryan Goetter, who had to sit out of the performance for medical reasons, cracked us all up and shattered the nervous atmosphere. From up in the stands I heard my dad yell, "Let's go *Bario-tones*!" to my brother, making fun of the misspelling on the back of our show shirts. I looked over to my left- Zach didn't even move, as if he hadn't heard it.

The drum majors saluted, and we scattered to our places.

The guard stretched over on their knees, posed to begin their dance.

We flexed our fingertips and got comfortable sitting cross-legged.

At this competition we might not have sounded quite as amazing as we were expecting to at the end of our season, but we played with heart. Despite a few stick-outs, flag drops, and missed dots, we threw our best effort into the performance and hoped our foot-stumbles and musical scrapes weren't fatal.

It was even evident as we left the field that we were feeling down. Without even knowing the results of the competition, most of us figured chances were slim that we could squeeze into finals and compete again later. In our minds, we didn't stand a chance against the giants performing after us. However, the sun was still shining and the air was still brilliantly fresh. I began to wonder if the wind was beginning to change for us.

Once back at the buses, we climbed aboard and did our best to change in the seats. Changing on a bus where one girl snaps angrily at any guys who dared turn around and accidentally glimpse hot-pink undergarments while her pals changed was tough. It was also stressful when the rest of the band tried awkwardly to ignore one another while balancing to cower in a seat and pull on a pair of jeans. The situation was quite difficult! Some of us dated within the band, but we all tried not to accidentally creep on one another while in public and accidentally make everyone miserable.

The parents set up a small lunch assembly line with sandwiches, fruit, chips, and drinks to take to the small grassy area by the bus. What could be more fun that sitting in the grass eating and laughing and having a picnic with more band kids?

"Save me a seat. I'm going to get a sno-cone."

"Me too!"

Krista and I shoved the blankets we were holding toward Mat and the others in my group and headed for the concession area. They paused at another stand before proceeding to our designated section of bleachers located behind the field.

We returned with red sno-cones and settled onto the cold bleacher benches next to our friends to watch the shows.

It wasn't nearly as fun as it could have been if we had seen the shows from the front, but it had its benefits sitting behind the shows: we got to see behind giant props and watch the people in black outfits crawl around pushing things like stone bridges and holding doors or giant umbrellas for the color guard to run behind and grab flags stashed in plastic garbage bins. (Very clever.)

It was also hard to hear the names of the shows whenever the announcer called them out, so we had a blast trying to guess the shows by interpreting the dancing and the music. One show with a stone bridge prop featured a guard soloist dressed in a Tinker Bell green dress, who then threw herself backward off the bridge through a nifty secret gate into waiting arms (which only we could see from the back). A shout-out to Rock Bridge Marching Band for having a hilarious color guard and marching ensemble that was a blast to talk to afterward, especially when we asked what their show was about. Tinker Bell wasn't really committing fairy-icide, we discovered. Their show was about *Bridge to Terabithia*, and it really was an excellent performance; it was sad to find out that they wouldn't be competing at GSL later in the season.

Aside from the disadvantages, we enjoyed the performances. Eventually the last band took the field for performance. The butterflies of anticipation descended. Drummers, guard, and horn line alike flooded back into the bleachers from the t-shirt booths and the concession stands.

We checked the time on our phones every few minutes and waited silently for the judges. Small conversations took place as students anticipated favorable or unfavorable scores.

"I feel pretty confident. I think we have a shot at making it into finals. I mean, we weren't perfect, but we did good. Even though, it *was* pretty cold," said Alfredo Deleon, a saxophone player.

If we make finals, we will be better.

We promise.

Padawan addressed us with the plans for the rest of the day, dependent upon our placement in the preliminaries and whether or not we make finals.

"Okay, guys, here's the plan. If we don't make finals, we'll pack up all the percussion equipment, load the buses and head out. If-" his eyebrows raised and his face lit up- "we make finals, which is unlikely because we are competing with the big guys, but not impossible, then we'll stay. *In that event,* we will draw times for performance, and stick around to watch everyone else perform and the final judging. Cool? Okay. Let's see how we did."

It felt like an eternity passed as we waited for the judges to finish the scoring and take a quick break before sending the results to the announcer. Searching the faces of those around me, I saw some with resignation; believing we didn't have a chance, that we essentially shipwrecked ourselves earlier that morning, they prepared to accept another band season of *almost* and *so close, but not quite there.*

And then I saw the few with hopeful eyes, the ones who believed change was in the air. *All of our work and aspirations could not boil down to nothing!*

We knew our strengths, and after reflecting, accepted our weaknesses as a silent challenge to be better. *Please*, we begged silently, *let us redeem ourselves.*

"We will now announce the scores," the announcer boomed over the loudspeakers.

Scores were traditionally read off from the smallest class to the largest class at most competitions. At this competition, it was just the awards for "Best Visual" or "Best Overall," and such along with placement. Numbers were not read aloud at most competitions, but were available for the directors on the judges' score sheets.

"Class A results:

"Outstanding Music…Marquette and Collinsville!"

We cheered.

"Outstanding Visual… Parkway West!"

"Outstanding General Effect…"

We held our breath.

"Collinsville!"

More cheering, but we held back a little. Getting awards doesn't guarantee a top-three placement.

"Third place…Parkway West!"

"Second place…Marquette!"

Holding my breath began to hurt.

"And first place…Collinsville!"

If any of the other bands screamed loud, we were positively *deafening*.

And there was still the list of finalist bands to listen for…

"The bands that will compete in Finals:

"Camdenton, Rock Bridge, Fort Zumalt South, Francis Howell, Jefferson City, Alton, St. Charles West, Frances Howell Central, Parkway South…"

I counted in my head. Nine. There was one spot left.

"…And Collinsville."

About sixty mouths dropped open. We leapt to our feet and screamed, shaking our section of bleachers.

Moments later, beaming, Mr. Padawan arrived to collect us to get ready to perform again.

Since many of us had assumed we wouldn't be performing again, few of us had eaten dinner yet. Walking back to the buses past all the food stands made stomachs rumble grumpily.

As we passed, I noticed a pizza stand that wasn't there before.

"Got any left?" someone asked.

"Plenty!" called the lady cheerfully.

"Save a few- *we'll be coming back!"*

At 6:10 p.m. (after Padawan drew a short straw at the judges' box for competing order), we waited to perform second. We got dressed quickly, did a condensed rapid factory drill, and then took half an hour to mentally prepare and focus on attacks and releases, which were some of our biggest challenges.

We had gotten our wish. Now the hunger for success and thirst for redemption bubbled within us. A marching band with something to prove was formidable competition.

The moment came to crowd onto the end zone and hear Padawan's final tips for us before taking the field and hopefully knocking our previous score clear out of the water. This time around, it was evident that we were in the game. Even move to move, dot to dot, we could feel the difference. We mopped up the messes from earlier and polished some of the rough patches into gleaming artwork.

We held our heads high as we marched off the field. As we marched back to the buses, glowing with confidence, whispers began to drift around us.

Game on.

Dressed back in our street clothes, we purchased a majority of the remaining pizzas and headed up to the stands to enjoy the rest of the competition.

We sat through a tuba player and a drum major duking it out on the field for a lady, space-age adventures, and a journey down a rabbit hole. All in all, it was as much fun to watch others participate in what we love to do as actually marching. They watched us perform, so we watched and cheered the others out of respect.

After the very last performance, the judges quickly submitted the final score to the announcer.

Padawan came to sit in our section for the results. Speaking quietly to us, he congratulated us on our evening performance.

"Whether or not we take home the gold, tonight, we were champions."

"In tenth place- Collinsville High School, with 65.5 points!"

The rest was history. Padawan congratulated us, saying that we did excellent, and that we had the smallest band in finals by far, but that we nearly caught up with the band in ninth place with less than a point separating us. In fact, between us and the first place winner who had 76.8 points, there was less than a twelve-point difference.

"You guys went out there and did your best. I'm proud of you all. Now, keep in mind that we're still getting better. Next week, between all the homecoming week madness, we'll address the problems from earlier and work on cleaning. *Oh my goodness, cleaning*!"

"At the Edwardsville competition, we sent a message. We told them we were contenders, you know, entering the ring, ready to fight for the championship. We've sent a message to the bands in our class that Collinsville isn't here to fill space this year. We were hunting, sneaking up from behind to earn our spot on the food chain. After tonight, *we are the hunted.* Those bands just had their wake-up call delivered to their front door with a smile! They're going to get better. *That* is our challenge."

It was no disappointment coming in tenth when we had a disadvantage in size (and therefore volume), because that was all that was holding us back from a fair challenge.

We were already looking forward to the next year's competitions. *Competitors beware if we get that large freshman class we hear rumors about…!*

Chapter 17: "A Nice Place to Be"

Homecoming Week: Monday, October 3-Thursday, October 6

The week began with a horde of bunny slippers, hair rollers, and extreme cases of bedhead on campus. Homecoming Week kicked off with Pajama Day on Monday and ended with Purple and White Pride Day on Friday, the day of the Homecoming Game, and the Homecoming Dance and Coronation on Saturday night.

Of course, after the school day, we had to change out of our pajamas and into athletic clothes. Everything that entered the practice field became caked with a layer of grimy dust and dirt by the time it left, soiled to the point of needing a good washing. This included instruments, and by the end of the season they had more dirt in the pads and valves than in the Egyptian pyramids. It wasn't wise to wear a favorite pair of sweats out to practice in the Dustbowl, as we had dubbed our dead practice field.

After the long weekend (and going to class in 'jammies'), we were kind of tired. It showed on the field.

Throughout the rehearsal on Monday, our feet and timing were stronger than the music on the field. After correcting a few problems, we began intense run-throughs of large chunks of the show over and over again.

"We've got more work to do, guys. We aren't there yet, but we will be. Right now, we're at a nice place to be."

Tuesday's school spirit antics spent our valuable rehearsal time. The Class Color Day competitions took place on our practice field where we usually rehearse and included a colorful menagerie of classmates participating in tug o'war, relays, and egg-toss. *An egg toss!* We all imagined in horror the possibility of having to step in dropped eggs on the move. (Eew!) Luckily, our responsible students in charge of the events cleaned up the messes and left, so practice started without a hitch other than beginning an hour late.

Wednesday was only slightly complicated. It was Famous Duo Day, so super heroes and blue-haired "things" joined the marching band for the day. None tripped over their capes. The few of us who wore face-paint and temporary hair color wiped our faces frequently to mop our melting personas out of our eyes. I would say that the rehearsal was 'super,' but that would be exaggerating a little…

Collinsville looked classy on Thursday. For Red Carpet Runway Day, the gentlemen wore suits or khakis and the ladies wore formal dresses and painfully glamorous high heels.

The parade started two hours after school ended, so getting to the warm-up spot quickly was essential. All the band and color guard stood in varying stages of dress throughout the room. While some of us paused to remove formal shoes, others had already changed in the bathrooms into athletic shorts and white t-shirts. Crowded into the back of the room between the timpani and stray tuba cases, the guard girls swarmed the mirrors to apply makeup and tease hair.

To the Homecoming Parade, there was no official transportation for the masses. Younger members had to carpool with older students and parents both to and from the parade. If someone had peeked into the back seat of a car, among shakos, instrument cases, and water jugs there might have been a few hidden band kids underneath everything. Whatever it took, we always found a way to get where we needed to go.

It was intensely hot. The winds rarely stirred, leaving the humid air to sit on us like a wool blanket in the sun. The grass in the empty lot where we warm up was freshly mowed; the severed blades flicked into the air, drifting around tickling our faces and sticking to the beads of sweat on our cheeks and brows. Sneezing spread like the twenty-four-hour flu as we began to set up our circle. It was a wretched time for those who had allergies.

It was pure nose-itching misery by the time the float covered with flowers cruised by.

"Ready? Band, set, *UP*!"

We snapped to attention, locking our instruments at the carry position, and stepped off when the drums began their cadences.

Bright shards of candy already littered the ground. Many children throwing candy from atop tall vehicles had trouble throwing it far enough to reach the sidewalk, leaving it right where we marched. Accidentally roll-stepping squarely on a jawbreaker was painful, although it wasn't half as bad as stepping in animal waste. (We were completely happy to step on candy instead of the alternative!)

One of the most important roles of the front row in parade marching was the constant visual communication between the drum majors and the marchers. The person at the center of the front row not only set the step size for the band and kept the lines evenly spaced, but also used eye signals and facial movements to guide the drum majors while they marched backwards to direct us. This parade route had several left turns, so it was a chore to make all the turns and keep signaling to Staci, who was in front of me.

As soon as we finished the parade, we lined the sidewalk to cheer on the middle school band for their final stretch. We screamed as obnoxiously loud as we could and made attempts to embarrass younger siblings. My sister (the oboe player), one of the mellophones, and a trombonist with older siblings in the band all blushed red as we screamed their names at the top of our lungs. We loved to support the middle-school band kids.

It came time to reload the instrument trailer and catch our rides back to school. The sky transformed rapidly into a dark stewing mess, grumbling angrily and spitting rain at the parade floats. Droplets ricocheted off of automobiles like rim shots on a snare drum.

Following a busy week of Homecoming antics, we had the big game performance and Senior Night the next evening, followed by the highly-anticipated McKendree marching band competition with the grassy hill and workshop with a marching pro.

The road we were traveling on, sticky with candy, was taking us somewhere quickly, be it great or disappointing. Time was disappearing fast.

Would there still be enough time to become all we aspired to be?

Chapter 18: Aww, Rats!

Friday, October 7, 2011- Homecoming Football Game

"K-K-K-A-H,
O-O-O-K-S,
K-A-H,
O-K-S,
Kahoks, Kahoks, KAHOKS!"

Our hard work despite the week's craziness paid off big-time. The stadium was ripping at the seams from the giant crowd that poured in to watch the game. Not only was it our big game of the year but also the last one on the old grass before breaking ground for the new turf stadium for next year.

Mr. Padawan prepared us for the evening at the after-school rehearsal. "Ignore the crowd. It's going to be huge, and you're going to be distracted. *They* don't exist."

He explained that we would have a lot of "hurry up and wait" going on. Senior Night, which occurred in all the athletic programs offered at Collinsville High School, was when the senior athletes give flowers to their parents after having their names called at the center of the room (or field) and say goodbye to the sport during half-time. For the band seniors, although we had two competitions and a parade left, it was an important night. It was the first step towards weaning us off our addiction to band and preparing us to eventually sever ourselves from the group.

Eventually, but not during Senior Night. For our band, it was the night to honor our supporters, parents and siblings who had given up hours of their time and the funds necessary to keep us doing what we love.

Per usual, we marched in and took our place in the band bleachers after performing our pre-show. At that moment we were grateful for our isolation; we had reserved seats which were apart from the rest of the crowd.

At the start of the second quarter we gathered our shakos and collected our nerves quietly, walking toward our places at the end-zone.

In the cool air, as we stood watching the football launch through the air and bugs zipping about in the beams of the lights above, time slowed for us. Different thoughts and memories played in our heads like news broadcasts: getting food at the concession stands and throwing tinfoil missiles at each other, running around with water balloons and joking with Padawan, and the golden moments of personal victory when we redeemed ourselves at Lafayette that night and cheering as though we had won first place in finals.

We had come a long way as a group and as a band family.

A minute remained on the clock.

"Football!"

A tuba player ducked and the clarinets and saxophones on the left side of the warm-up arch dove to avoid a stray football. It sailed over Padawan's head and barely missed the drum majors.

The seconds on the clock dripped away and the football players took the field for their senior ceremony. Cameras flashed like blinking arcade lights as the families of the athletes cried or smiled next to their sons.

Then it was our turn. The small handful of seniors smiled and posed for pictures.

Kayla couldn't wait for the moment to pass. "I was focused on the performance. We still had a show to put on, you know. I was thinking, hey, can we go now?"

There was less than ten minutes on the half-time countdown.

"Watch the drum majors. They will signal you to finish and exit the field when we run out of time. We probably won't get to perform the entire show." Mr. Padawan ushered us onto the field.

This time, when we took the field, it seemed like we were moving in slow motion. The crowd seemed bigger than ever, and the lights seemed even brighter!

Since the beginning of band camp, we had grown and learned. The same kids who worried more at first about wrapping themselves around boyfriends and girlfriends during break or putting on makeup and wearing fancy hairdos now valued their time sweating and working extremely hard with their best friends. We learned a lesson or two about belonging and being accepted on the field and about putting personal feelings aside for the love of marching. Mr. Padawan learned something about us: that training us to give one hundred and ten percent of ourselves on the field and to be satisfied with nothing less than our best could have incredible results and give us confidence in ourselves. Almost as important as having the training and ability to perform that way was making us *believe* we could.

"It was an honor to be a part of the program and to finish my senior year as a drum major. I felt accomplished to be standing here after four years and performing as a drum major for the first time in the stadium here as a senior," said Molly. For the final time on our football field, Kayla took her place on the podium and Molly and Staci joined us on the field.

Everything went right. The movements flowed

together flawlessly with our body moves and formations greatly improved. The music seemed to pack quite a punch for the audience- the spectators didn't quiet to silence, but the noise level dropped significantly. They were watching.

Marching felt like gliding. The cool air danced around our ankles and brushed across our cheeks with a tickling breeze.

At the end of the third movement, the audience rewarded us with a generous applause. It was over too soon; we were out of time because of the senior ceremonies. Despite our unfinished business and the fact that we had never gotten to perform the whole show on the move on our own field, we marched back off the field with dignity and pride.

Stranger events took place that made our exit memorable.

Promptly after the finish of our third movement, we turned and marched off the opposite way from taking the field.

Danielle and I were two of the last people off the field due to our dots where we left off at the far left of the field. While following the crowd, Danielle gasped and stumbled, bumping into me.

"Something ran over my foot!" she whispered.

We stopped walking for a moment and turned around to look.

A big, fat brown rat waddled around on the edge of the field. The rest of the band already seated in the bleachers pointed and laughed at it. It was definitely the size of my size-eight marching shoe, if not bigger…

And I thought the drummers were considered the local wildlife…!

Near the front gates, a man asked Alyssa if she could run inside and rescue "Squeakers" for him. When she told the guard girls, they laughed at the expression on her face. Leah, the dance soloist in the third movement, noted that she thought she had seen something moving near her feet during her dance.

The rat eventually escaped into the night, gone but not forgotten at the Collinsville football field.

The game was close and lively, but it ended in a loss for the Kahoks. Regardless of the ending score, the memories and achievements recognized lingered on after the football teams shook hands, the crowds emptied the stands, and we stowed our instruments safely away until the next competition.

The only regret we took from the performance was that we couldn't perform the last two movements for our peers on Collinsville territory.

The next challenge for us was to perform the whole show, for better or worse, at competition with all the recent body and horn moves added in.

Let's bring home a trophy.

Chapter 19: "A Collinsville State of Mind"

Saturday, October 8, 2011- McKendree Marching Band Preview of Champions

It was cold outside. Cold, and dimly lit.

Slowly the temperature rose, like icicles gradually dripping away in the morning sun after a freeze. The sun broke through the trees and clouds to make its appearance just as we climbed up the stairs and began to suit up for the competition.

In a double arch formation on the concrete, we wiggled our fingers and toes to keep warm. Since it was so cold, we were having a full-dress rehearsal with our jackets on. They weren't very thick, but they kept out some of the chills of the biting wind.

Behind me, the trumpets buzzed their lips to relieve their chops. So far, we were having a decent morning. The sun's rays banished most of the chill after it had risen high into the sky above the trees, bathing the sidewalks and concrete in its soft orange hues.

Mr. Padawan informed us that this rehearsal would be brief. "We'll have time to get warmed up once we arrive. Right now, we need to have a quick air-only run of each chunk of music, then *one* repetition playing. Let's not make this difficult. We'll hit the hard sections and clean up where we must. I plan for us to be on the buses to leave in a little over an hour."

Throughout September and October, the two elements of our show had played tug-of-war for the perfect balance. Visual and music had suffered and thrived alternating weeks, much to our frustration. *Can't we have both elements cleaned?*

And just when we thought we were finally getting everything, another horn move or body move was added. For the first time at competition, we planned to add in our box "ripple effect" in the fourth movement that scared the bejeebies out of us.

Only the performance would tell whether we were ready, if no dots were missed, no body moves were late, and no flags were dropped.

Everything was halfway calm on the forty-five minute ride to McKendree University; we were trying to keep our composure watching a freshman brass player eat a lemon peel and trying to handle singing our parts with the rest of the sections on the bus.

Kayla was trying to keep things under control from the front of the bus. Much to the dismay of the flute and clarinets, Molly and Staci were on the other bus, so Kayla did her best to direct us through the first three movements (painfully and obnoxiously loud with the spare energy of excited band kids) until we all miscounted in the fourth and de-railed. After that –ten minutes into the bus ride –we all gave up singing it.

"Section leaders, run through your parts with your sections. Make sure everyone has their gloves and gauntlets with them." Kayla sat down and the different sections all began to work…except the flutes and clarinets.

We weren't the only orphan sections. Dominick and John also rode on the "cool" percussion bus- the one with fewer people and no singing going on. Rachel looked at me, sharing my confusion. Trevor had ear buds in, and Katelyn and Danielle were in their own little worlds.

"Kayla?" I asked. "What do we do?"

"Just do your best," she told me.

Maybe it was for the best that we just chilled and tried to enjoy the ride.

The campus at McKendree was fairly large and beautiful. We were led between two apartment buildings to a grassy common area to warm up. Several of our former members were attending McKendree (mostly music majors), so we expected to run into Kahok alumni frequently throughout the day.

The McKendree Preview of Champions was judged by band size and divided into six categories. Since we shrunk in size by several members from last year, we became small enough to move from the fourth class to the third smallest class. The competition was split in half (the smallest three compete and the largest three compete) with separate awards ceremonies. Instead of performing in the evening like last year, we had a mid-morning slot almost right before the awards ceremony. Unlike Lafayette or Edwardsville, this competition also awarded trophies for Best Visual, Best Music, Outstanding General Effect, Best Percussion, and Best Guard per class, as well as a trophy for the Grand Champion with the highest score in each half. This competition would be the one to tell us where we truly were by our scores. Many of the bands that competed here competed at GSL.

We prepared for our performance with the usual routine. A couple of McKendree students stood nearby, watching us as we warmed up.

Something felt a little off with us. We were excited and had plenty of physical energy for the show, but we were somewhere else mentally. The pressure of competition was getting to us.

"Let's get it together, guys. Put energy through your feet." Padawan caught traces of our wandering attention throughout the morning exercises. "Pay attention to phrases! Go all the way to the cutoff- you *have* to look good without sacrificing the way you play. In fact..." He paused for dramatic effect. "You guys are all ugly. Sound good." A few people giggled as he gave us one of his humorous signature looks.

We took a walk on the wild side to proceed to the field for performance- *literally*. One of the bands we passed had its guard in leopard-print outfits. On our other side, a band had cavemen and similarly dressed girls. Both bands looked like fierce competition.

Looking back, we felt and *looked* cocky. The way we stepped across the dry pavement and scraped our shoes over loose pebbles, the way our jaws were slack and not set with any sort of determination at the time- we looked like we were about to let everything we had worked for slip by.

It was too late when we got onto the field. Problems began to smack us in the faces from the first note. Flags fell and notes cracked. The music sounded choppy from the unison of our breathing. The mouthpiece of Sean, a sophomore baritone player, went flying over his shoulder the same exact way that Jordan's did at the first football game. Later, a judge returned Sean's mouthpiece to Padawan. Several leads in the brass sections played too loud in their attempts to play hero and save our performance. It wasn't terrible by high school marching standards, but it certainly wasn't what we believe our best was or what we practiced.

After leaving the field, we were taken inside to a brief clinic sponsored by McKendree with a professional judge critiquing our performance. Notably, he complimented our matching flags and guard outfits and commended the practical choice of colors corresponding to our show.

"You would find it crazy," he told us, "how many bands have flags, props, and uniforms that have nothing to do with the show and make the whole performance confusing.

Among the frequent mistakes pointed out by the judge was the amount of "stick-outs." At times, there was a significant difference between the volume contributed by the majority of the sections and the few leads who could hit the highest notes loudly that we could *clearly* hear when the footage of our performance was played back for us in a medium-sized theater room.

Similar to what Padawan had worked on with us all week, the judge brought up other issues with phrasing and the gaps where we all took breaths. Nothing said was untrue in the least; everything exposed by our judge needed attention.

Mr. Padawan was frustrated. "That wasn't how you perform when we rehearse. It seemed like you were going through the motions, but the focus and intent was lost."

Such was the pride of Collinsville: worse than tangled shoelaces, it threatened to trip up our entire season and everything we had gained and worked hard for.

Padawan did not sugarcoat his words. "I'm disappointed. Everything I've said, everything we worked on, went in one ear and straight out the other. Guys, playing hard music means hard work. It means nothing if we try and fail. The only way we are going to take GSL, to have a memorable season, and to become *champions*, is by trying and *succeeding*."

His disappointment echoed through the band. We were more than a little disappointed in ourselves. He was right- that performance was *nothing* like any of the rehearsals after school that frequently receive compliments for our discipline and precision. As he walked us to our spot on the big grassy hill near the bleachers back inside the complex, he turned to us and said, "Honestly, that performance doesn't deserve to win today. One of the other groups is going to take first, and we may not even place. We have practice all next week. Come prepared for hard work and a lot of cleaning."

Sullenly, we trudged over to the hill, hot and tired. We were more upset at ourselves than anything, dreading the whole awards ceremony.

I elbowed my brother before sitting down. "Do you think we have a chance?"

"I have no idea."

The first awards ceremony, for bands 1A, 2A, and 3A, began solemnly with a prickly, electric atmosphere. The entire band was on edge, prepared for the worse, but still daring to hope for the best.

The announcer quickly announced the awards for classes 1A and 2A. Grass rustled as we waited restlessly for our fate.

"In third place…Windsor High School!"

I could see our drum majors standing exposed in the line-up for our class. I could not see their expressions but wondered with the rest of the band what they were thinking.

"In second place…Mater Dei!"

Nick, the tuba player sitting to the left of me, was staring ahead intently. Two of the clarinet players sitting nearby had their mouths set in grim lines.

At that moment, the whole Collinsville band was wearing a frown. The word for those moments of doubting ourselves and our capabilities is *misery.* Nothing was worse than disappointment in ourselves after reflecting on all the hours and effort we put into this sport we love.

Regardless of this performance, resolution to shape up individually and as a team was written in the air.

Mental energy. Focus. Intent. Find the Collinsville state of mind.

Collinsville had a renewed thirst for redemption.

"In first place…COLLINSVILLE HIGH SCHOOL!"

As soon as we processed the announcer's words we shot up off the grass and became a cluster of screaming, laughing and jumping wild animals.

Victory meant something else to us from that moment on, especially because the announcer wasn't quite finished…

"Best Music goes to…Collinsville!"

"Best Visual goes to…Collinsville!"

"Outstanding General Effect goes to…Collinsville!"

"Best Percussion goes to…Collinsville!"

"Best Guard goes to…Collinsville!"

"And, the Grand Champion of the class 1A through 3A caption goes to...Collinsville High School!"

We almost danced back to the bus, scattering rocks in the dusty pavement as we went. Kayla, Molly, and Staci were all smiles.

Mr. Padawan climbed up into the bus. Unsure of what he would say, we quieted quickly.

"Guys...don't be proud. Okay, okay, this is your thing, don't gloat," he added, looking at our innocent crocodilian grins. "At GSL, these things will *kill* your score. You've got to admit, though," he paused, allowing a smile to break through his terrifyingly serious band-director look for our benefit, "it's pretty amazing that, despite how terrible that performance was compared to our rehearsals, we swept *everything.* These bands are going to be out for blood now, figuratively, so we can't rest on our laurels. Alright guys...see you Monday."

We cheered.

Our work was clearly cut out for us. The biggest challenge we faced before GSL was not defeating any particular band or fixing any real devastating messes. Our biggest challenge would be overcoming our own pride and re-focusing on the prize.

It was time to become a team again, just in time for our final competition in two weeks.

Part 4: Ascent

Chapter 20: On Fire

Tuesday, October 11, 2011

In the first two days of rehearsal since McKendree, we made incredible progress in all areas.

Cleaning was the name of the game. (Clean and repeat. Clean and repeat. It never ended.)

Intense focus was put on feet and the formation first. Each movement was cleaned in chunks, run once or twice for adjustments, and then repeated several more times to make the changes stick. "There's no time to waste on the sections we have already cleaned. We *need* to keep moving; competition is just around the corner. GSL is next Saturday, guys. Time is running out."

Along with the cleaning regimen, Padawan resolved to make the most of every rehearsal. Not a moment was wasted. The way we would measure our efficiency would be by whether or not we improve at the end of each rehearsal from the previous day.

Each section was getting better from repetition to repetition. There were fewer silly mistakes and goof-ups showing up on the field. When they did pop up, however, they were a much bigger deal. There was no room for error anymore.

"This run could be how it goes at GSL. It had better be good."

We needed to be ready.

On Tuesday, the last half hour of the rehearsal expired with a streak of killer one-and-done chunks. Each chunk had one air-only run, then one with sound. Pow! We were showing our *show* who was boss.

From the lift, Padawan's huge grin was clearly visible to us.

"Guys… if you just play like this next Saturday…you're going to be unstoppable. Just think…we've got another week to prepare for the competition, and you're already this good. You're going to scare the *crap* out of the other bands."

We all paused to imagine this before heading out for the evening.

Now that the season was winding down, we savored the remaining moments of our practices with a greedy possessiveness like that of a child hoarding the last remaining candy bars from trick-or-treating on Halloween. It was not that the hard work was over and it would be all laughs and fun; no, we were just so used to the hard work, and loved our show so much that we would miss it dreadfully and wouldn't quite know what to do with ourselves when it ended. Until then, we were determined to put everything we had into finishing this exciting, crazy, eventful and unexpected season with something memorable. We *could not* settle for maybe or almost; no, we need a *never before* and something we have never dared to hope for yet to satisfy us.

We had improved so much since the beginning of the season.

Unfortunately, Mother Nature wasn't about to make things easy for us.

Chapter 21: "Here Comes the Rain Again"

The Week before GSL

After all the challenges endured and efforts made to make our show what it was, chaotic forces beyond our control decided to meddle. Mother Nature came to town adorned in her thickest gray gown and packed with enough rainy, windy fury to cripple our last week of rehearsal.

The forecast called for several days of rain throughout the week. We only had a few rehearsals left to maintain and polish the show for our very last performance. On Monday, it wasn't a crisis yet. We simply held rehearsal inside, adjusting and cleaning much of the music in movements four and five. Outside, the already-crisp temperatures plummeted steadily.

We squashed the urge to panic about the weather. Winding down to the end of a successful season, we had already surpassed our own expectations. Somehow, there was a tiny bit of reassurance for us. Something told us that we would be okay. *The rain will eventually let up, and the sun will shine again.*

Tuesday brought a new wave of trials, little injuries to our confidence and thorns to slash our morale. A dark cloud dropped anchor over the high school and drizzled cold rain continuously throughout the day. There was still no chance of using the field, muddy and speckled with puddles, so we were forced to bundle up and practice on the asphalt student parking lot.

Extra pairs of sweatpants were rationed among students, as well as long-sleeved shirts and extra jackets. The rehearsal was going to be far from enjoyable, but we needed it and we *knew* it. We pulled on our uniform gloves to offer a little warmth to our clammy fingers, chilled from the cold and the rain.

For the first time, we missed the blistering heat of July during band camp and the ability to feel sensation in our fingertips.

We practiced smartly. There was little time spent standing still. Instead, we switched between forward, backward, and sideways exercises and cleaning large chunks of our music.

Our toes and fingers got a little cold, but at the end of rehearsal, we were satisfied. Nothing was about to stop us from ending the season our program had hoped for without a fighting chance to win.

"Take care of yourselves, guys. Don't get sick after practice. Wear layers; wear your gloves, hats, whatever it takes. We can't afford to miss opportunity, so we need to be smart when we rehearse."

It was hard to focus and put out our best efforts with cold limbs, but we managed to push past it and maintain our ability to play well on the move under pressure. It was much too late in the game to slip back into old habits or to get sloppy and lazy.

"Rain, rain, go away, don't come back 'til after Saturday…"

Fingers and toes throbbed. Wind whipped loose strands of hair across our faces. And there was *still* a blanket of wet, gray clouds draped overhead tossing cold water droplets like confetti. Wednesday was shaping up to be just as terribly awful as the days before.

Unlike the weather, we were still improving, little by little.

Mr. Padawan gave us our final horn moves and body moves for the show. It was like the strange sensation of accomplishment followed by sadness when putting the final piece in a jigsaw puzzle. You survey your work, gaze at the puzzle, and eventually begin a new puzzle.

When we walked away from that rehearsal, we had strength, dedication, and pride. Doing something that many others never get the chance to experience was an incredible joy that could not be replaced. Marching and performing fast, riveting shows and knowing we had pulled it off fed our souls with confidence and energy that made the few moments actually spent performing for competitions linger on.

How successful the final moments would be would rely on the results of the next two days' final rehearsals.

"If you keep up this effort…no band will come anywhere *near* you."

Chapter 22: The Final Countdown

Friday, October 21, 2011

The sky was overcast: featureless, gray and expansive like a sheet of dingy ice frozen across the heavens. It was chilly outside, but there was no rain.

We bundled up to go outside. Musicians with metal instruments puffed their warm breath into frigid mouthpieces. Few students dared to brave the winds without sweatpants, which added to the warmth provided by our uniform jackets and gloves we were wearing to get us used to how our performance would feel at GSL.

On Thursday, during concert band, the ordinary brown side table was pulled away from the wall and to the front of the room.

Mr. Padawan began the class by gesturing grandly to it. "Does everyone see this table?"

We mumbled *yes* and sat there, fidgeting or attempting to finish homework on our stands. It was just a table.

"It's...*empty*. There is nothing on it. Now, remember that the trophies from McKendree *were* on the table. They're up on the shelf now. That's over, and done. We need to focus on our performance this Saturday. We have to go out there, play hard, and earn it. So!" He clapped his hands together. "Let's bring home the hardware!"

It was a short and powerful speech to rally us for the finish we've been working for.

We left the band room as completely wired adrenaline junkies that afternoon, more than a little excited for the final competition in just two days.

Our noses ran and our cheeks flushed pink.

We hardly noticed. We were busy in the land of one-and-dones and knock-'em-deads. It seemed like everything was lining up perfectly for the finish we'd dreamed of for our season. Reflecting upon the competition results in the years before Padawan was director, the seniors were thrilled to have a shot at winning.

"We didn't win before he came, not for years. This is new," said Dominick. He especially was eager to end his senior season with a first for the Collinsville marching band.

The fourth movement body moves, which had been a messy effect for the longest time, were finally lining up. The even rows that had a sudden sideways lunge (after spinning around to face the front) finally hit their dots, eliciting a pleased response from Mr. Padawan. The crisp visual lines essential to our general effect (G.E.) score would increase our chances of winning our class at GSL.

Our sole focus, in all areas, was to try and match or exceed what bands bigger than us were capable of on the field. To even compare with the grand semi-truck giants with multiple directors and big budgets, we had to seem big. To do this, we shocked other bands by starting our show sitting down. Then, we blew everyone away with our sound for our size. The knockout punch required pushing ourselves until we *became* our show. We were *Solaris.* We had to be elegant machines to change our record and prove what we could do.

"You guys have proven how badly you want it- I can see it when you march. The focus is there! If you keep this up, we're going to go out there and do our best." Mr. Padawan said before our final run-through of the day, our last before the official day of competition. “Full run-through. *March like this is it.* Perform like this is the last time you will play this show.” He switched off the mic.

The air was still; the ground was frosted and the birds were gone.

A driving tribal beat interrupted the stillness without warning. An ancient dance turned into radiant light; light turned into time; time turned into a savage turmoil. Fingers flickered like fire, burning through the chaotic runs. Then the chaos turned to glory.

In the vast, seemingly endless stretch of clouds, there was one tiny break that allowed the sunlight to shine down on us and briefly illuminate our striking sun feature. The guard gracefully glided into the half-circle formation in front of our arch, extending their shimmering golden swing flags to their sides to mirror the glowing orb peeking down from the heavens. Our sound began to rise off the field, above the building, and into the sky as our huge final chords engulfed the school and filled the air.

“Yes! Yes! That’s it! Keep going!”

Before the music continued after movement three, I noticed a butterfly struggling against the wind near the front sideline. The yellow-flecked brown and orange creature was battered with gusts of wind and tossed left and right. It finally escaped and landed on the red thirty-five yard line marker, where it stayed until the end of the run-through when woodwinds ran near to get water and it fluttered away. Like that butterfly battling its surroundings to get where it was going, we were fighting all our oppressors- funding, attendance, and time- and *achieving.*

All these opposing forces spiraled back into chaos,

spinning us in circles and throwing us in all directions with the apocalyptic finale.

We stood there breathless. A thick cloud of dirt poisoned our first gasping breaths, causing the majority of the band to cough and spit out the same dirt that was caked between instrument keys and inside valves and bells.

"Bring it in."

We crowded around the lift, talking anxiously among ourselves.

"Guys, bring it in and get quiet. C'mon." Dominick quieted us as we gathered around.

"C'mon guys, finish strong!" John added. This final pep-talk would set our attitudes for our early-morning GSL performance.

"Shhh!"

Mr. Padawan waited for silence.

"Let me talk to you a little bit about DCI Finals Week every year, in August, before band camp happens. All the drum corps in the world assemble in Indianapolis, Indiana, and they have like, four days of nothing but all-day rehearsals."

We looked around among ourselves, wondering where this was leading.

"And in those four days, there are drum corps that plateau; there are drum corps that, in fact, get worse; and there are the drum corps that rise to the top. Do you follow me?"

Kind of.

"And I'm telling you, you guys remind me of a drum corps that is rising to the top."

"Whoo!" Our tuba player just couldn't contain his enthusiasm.

"The drum corps that is not going to *settle* for what they did a week ago; the drum corps that is not going to *settle* for coasting to the end. And you're being put in such a hard position, because of the weather.

"But it's not compromising anything- because with you guys, it's mind over matter. With you guys, it's training: believing in your training and believing in what you guys do great. And if you continue to do that, there will be a championship in your future."

This time more of us cheered.

"Because nobody *-nobody-* is going to sound how you sound. People have been saying that since Edwardsville. And we weren't at this level at Edwardsville. People have been saying that the whole time. And I was like, 'Ehh, we're not there yet, blah blah blah.' *Dude, no really, you guys are going to be ridiculous.* 'Ehh, we'll get there eventually, blah blah blah.' Well, we're *there*. And it's time to throw it down."

"I am so ridiculously excited. I can't *stand* it. And I hope you guys feel the same way. You guys did a great job, and you took care of your bodies. Do that again tonight: go home and drink water, eat chicken noodle soup, drink some orange juice. Please, please, *please* take care of yourselves, get plenty of rest, because we have to be on fire tomorrow. Yes?"

"Yeah!" We screamed, grinning and clapping.

"Get out of here. Very proud of you."

"Time for a bowl of chili!" Dominick yelled, walking off with my brother. I lingered there for a moment, then left.

Never before had I felt like I belonged on a team of any kind, until now.

So what happens after we perform? Will it be everything we worked for?

And afterwards, regardless of the results, where do we go from there?

Chapter 23: The Darkness Before Dawn

Saturday, October 22, 2011- The Greater Saint Louis Marching Competition

The sun was not yet up.

It was 6:23 a.m. when everyone began to arrive at the high school. The Earth was blanketed in darkness, the air was a chilly and smarting forty degrees Fahrenheit. We were eventually let inside, teeth chattering while exchanging quiet conversation.

This was it, the day we worked for all season.

It was an odd, still quiet in the band room, with only muted conversations and low whispers. No one was sure whether to be excited or nervous, happy or sad. This sport- this creation that sucked up every spare ounce of energy we possessed, every feeling that we held, every thought that crossed our minds for the past three months- was as much a part of us as the individual personality that lives within each of us, and it was about to end.

Personally, I was calm, tired, and anxious; there was at least forty minutes to kill before the rehearsal started. I disappeared while the others had their "Breakfast Club" meeting on top of the lockers to wrestle with my contacts and mentally prepare for the competition.

The exclusive "Breakfast Club" included my brother Zach, Dominick, and horn sergeant John. The morning of GSL (The Greater Saint Louis Marching Festival), they arrived early and ate their breakfasts while perched on top of the lockers, right next to the large windows with slanted blinds. *Apparently* it was a prestigious little group to participate in…

Molly, our most soft-hearted drum major, had yet to cry. Each time a freshman approached and started to say, “Molly, I’ll miss-,” she would cut them off and snap, “I’m not leaving *yet*!” and smile tightly. “Okay?” She told me later that she was saving her tears for after the competition. Staci and Kayla had true blood and guts inside, but we all swore Molly had stuffing like a teddy bear.

By the time I got those pesky contacts in, more students had arrived. Unlike before other competitions, the band room was bursting with a heavy, quiet stillness, and was only disturbed by subdued mumbling and the *click, click, snap* of instrument cases opening. No one played a note. Most wiped sleep from their eyes and yawned widely as they wandered around the band room or sat sprawled on the floor.

It was all too weird.

At 7:00 a.m. it was still dark.

We transformed into a busy, swarming mass as we set a circle in the band room. John took extra time with each stretch and warm-up exercise, releasing some of the anxiety from our systems.

“Get a good stretch, guys. As soon as the sun comes up we are heading outside.”

Half an hour later, we shivered as we walked onto our practice field for the final field rehearsal of the season.

It was a dry cold. There was very little moisture in the air to slow the bone-chilling gusts of wind. Once more we stood with goose bumps on our skin in the silence. It wasn’t so much the absence of sound that made a difference, but the presence of listening between us that supported our confidence.

The sun climbed over the treetops and up into the

sky as we finished our cycle of run and repeat, air-only, then play and repeat through all the chunks of the show. Everything took one playing run each- no retakes necessary.

Our final run was the icing on the cake.

We were ready.

Released to go eat and change, I sat with a group of underclassmen settled in the hallway, eating and chatting with the occasional grape or water bottle rolling over to another group and causing mischief. There were whispered worries and hopes throughout the meal.

Will we win? Will we do our best? Will we fail ourselves?

After eating, many of us went outside to help the pit load the truck. The remaining members got into half-uniform and checked their shakos, gloves, gauntlets, and jackets. The positive morning rehearsal calmed the nerves of *most* of us on the field, but not everyone…

After *eons* of loading, waiting, and last minute bathroom breaks, we loaded the buses. Molly and Staci were on our bus, the second bus, while Kayla and Padawan rode the notoriously calmer first bus with the pit, drum line, guard, and baritone sections.

Then, finally, we were off.

I took advantage of the chance to talk with Molly and Staci on the way to the competition.

"Hey, Staci, how do you feel?"

"Oh…uhhh…"

Molly jumped in. "I am *so* ready for this!"

"So excited." Staci echoed.

"-ready to kick major butt…"

Staci smiled. "I am so excited to just leave everything I have out on the field."

"What are you going to take away from this season?" I asked.

"I have changed so much this year, and I've become a lot stronger."

Molly agreed with Staci.

"I'm stronger, *you're* stronger… this season has really had its trials, and we've all pulled through it and came out better than we thought we would. It's amazing."

A short while later, we pulled into a dusty gravel parking lot crowded with school buses and charter buses. This was it.

The first step off the bus and onto the ground jolted us; from now on, we were in game mode. We would prove ourselves and leave many years' worth of dreams on the field, or go home without the gold. Either way, we were going to return to Collinsville knowing that there was nothing more we could have done.

The band parents were set up near the bus with boxes of energy bars, waters, and our black feather plumes stuffed into cardboard paper towel tubes. As quickly as we moved through the line and gobbled our snacks, it was go-time. In two neat lines behind the drum majors, John Bailey led the brass and I led the woodwinds across several streets to the entrance of the Edward Jones Dome.

We were led quietly around the Dome to somewhere separate from the actual stadium. With our steps echoing and squeaking in an even rhythm, we walked through a long, curving concrete tunnel: the walk through the hall of champions.

Our guide stopped us in a large concrete room that resembled the interior of a parking garage (minus the cars). For over half an hour we drilled different factory exercises, pushing through nerves and general anxiety to check our feet timing and step sizes one last time.

Next, we were walked to what looked like conference rooms, or banquet rooms- big carpeted rooms with huge room dividers and a few columns standing throughout the room. In this room, we were allowed to stretch and chill out for roughly ten minutes and alleviate some of our tension.

And then it was time for one final warm-up and tuning sequence before putting on the rest of our uniforms and heading to the turf.

My heart pounded like racehorses thundering across a racetrack as we stood waiting past the goal zone on the left side of the field. Band parent volunteers in the background pushed percussion instruments and the podiums into place, following the green tractor hauling the large marimbas into place.

"Don't look at that band. Look at me." Padawan whispered. A band from St. Louis was finishing up their city-traffic themed show.

We glued our eyes to our band director.

"This is it. This is the time to prove yourselves. Think about all we have accomplished for our program this year! We've come a long way; now it's time to go out there and show them what Collinsville can do!"

The applause for the band ahead of us exiting the

field interrupted him. Mr. Padawan motioned for us to face forward, towards the field, and then walked ahead of us like a general leading his soldiers to battle.

He turned, and left us with one final piece of advice:

"Leave it *all* on the field, everything you have."

Everything happened so fast.

We avoided looking at the giant television screen as Mr. Padawan had ordered- it was delayed and would mess up our timing. Instead, we stared at our drum majors as they saluted, while we marched to the fifty-yard line, paced off our spots, and sat down on shaky legs, all the while focusing on the drum majors to forget our own fears.

It was time to perform *Solaris* one last time as we never had before.

Everything happened in what seemed like a single moment.

The pounding pulse of the drum began, leaving us only an instant to glace up at the crowd. I steeled my shaky nerves and counted.

We began to dance.

The hypnotic music pulled at us. In that moment, when the world around us blurred, we ceased to worry and think. The sound grew with intensity, announcing the rising of the sun and the rising of our aspirations.

"*This year, we can do it. We can be unstoppable. We can win this!*"

Flags the color of the sun glimmered in the light. They nearly glowed with the accumulating dreams and energy poured into the entire season.

Everything comes down to this performance.

The melody swelled from our instruments and filled the air around us. Its ghostly echoes soared high above us. Everything felt smooth, like it was natural, like it was exactly as it should have been.

"After tonight, we are the hunted! Are you ready to rise to the challenge?"

The chaos and uncertainty of a long season melted in the booming final notes of the show. As our last sounds faded, we stood in the wake of our show different than we had been before we entered the stadium.

There we stood, despite all the challenges of the season, like champions.

That was how it happened. Pulses pounding, breath shaking, lips trembling, we stood moments later: silent, sad, and *jubilant* at the same time.

I picked out many of the band families from the crowd. My sister was practically jumping up and down, screaming at full capacity.

The air was different when we left: shattered by our performance. The thick veil of worries and the shadow of our own struggles were sliced to ribbons.

We managed to keep ourselves calm and contained until we got back to one of the concrete side areas, chattering anxiously about it. As far as my knowledge and limited view of the whole show was aware, there were few, if any, noticeable mistakes; our music, body moves, and formations were the cleanest they had ever been. Not one member or tech was able to suppress a grin…except Padawan.

His speech to us was brief. And before he said anything, he thanked us.

Mr. Padawan thanked us for an incredible season.

We didn't think to thank him for what he helped us do, but I suspect he knew how we felt.

"No matter what happens, whether or not we sweep the awards or take nothing- you went out there, and you threw it down. The ball was in your court, and you took it!"

"*Whether or not we win…today, we are champions.*"

Chapter 24: Rise

"No matter what happens, whether or not we sweep the awards or take nothing- you went out there, and you threw it down. The ball was in your court, and you took it!"

"Whether or not we win... today, we are champions."

"And the Outstanding Musical Performance award in the Blue Division goes to… Collinsville!"

The bleacher section jumped to its feet with a thunderous burst of cheering. The applause died out as we gripped our seats and sweated nervously. The announcer paused before continuing.

"And the Outstanding Visual Performance goes to…. Collinsville!"

More loud screams. To my left, my younger sister Abby, a hopeful guard member next year, screamed herself hoarse.

"And the Best General Effect goes to… Parkway West!"

We clapped politely while they enjoyed their moment- they had easier music than we did, but their action-packed show, *The Bourne Trilogy*, with scaffolds and wild leaps and exciting guard chase scenes, was certainly vivid.

Abby blurted, "It's because they had the car!" (There was a pedal-car as one of their moving props, new since the McKendree performance.)

"Now for the top five scores:

"In fifth place- Marquette High School!"

"In fourth place- Aurora High School!"

"In third place- Windsor High School!"

Every member of the Collinsville Band and their families held their breath collectively.

"In second place- Parkway West High School!"

The tension of our section squeezed and squeezed, our breaths held locked inside our chests-

"And the winner of the first place trophy in the Blue Division, with a score of 74.45- *Collinsville High School*!"

The air split with our triumphant yells and clapping and the crying of emotional seniors. The atmosphere in the Edward-Jones Dome was filled with something of pure brilliance, something beyond the awards and our pride.

It was triumph- not over other bands, color guards, drum lines, pits- but inside of ourselves. For the first time in over forty years, Collinsville had taken first at its final, and toughest, competition of the season. We worked harder than ever before, achieving a greatness of performance and a greatness of heart. The "little guys" proved that even with a smaller number of players, it was possible to take down Goliath with strength of sound and heart.

Awards ended; we poured out of the exits and onto the street outside. Dominick Viviano, the graduating senior baritone-player, didn't have to say much- his ear-to-ear grin had it covered. He hugged my brother, his second in command for two years, and tears welled up in his eyes.

"We did it."

Later, in the car, I smiled in triumph after thinking about the season. "Zach, I told you I could do it. Didn't you bet something?"

He looked up from the game he was playing. "You know, I don't always bet people to win. Sometimes I bet people to motivate."

All the hours of practice and performance throughout the season melted away as though it had been only minutes of time. With the season's end ushered in a long and busy winter color guard and drum line season, the competitive period for both concert bands, and unexpected events that altered the fate of the Collinsville High School Band program forever.

With the guidance and supervision of Rob Elston, the 2011 winter drum line won first place in Scholastic B at championships. The winter guard also had a very successful season under the supervision of Alyssa Greene.

In March of 2012, only a few weeks after the completion of the new turf field and replacement of the scoreboards and goalposts, we received an exciting message from Nike (yes, the shoe company!) asking to film us in a brief part of a commercial on the new turf field. The next week, we were excused from several hours of class to report to the field in uniform to be filmed. After a lot of waiting and hanging out while they laid out the temporary wooden track for the moving action camera, we took the shot about eleven times, and then it was all done. (It was one of the coolest things ever that Zach will always be jealous of, because only people sixteen and older could participate for legal reasons, and he was months away from being old enough.) The commercial, titled "I Would Run to You," aired during a commercial break on April 3, 2012, and is available to watch on various internet sites.

The Wind Ensemble, Symphonic Band, and Jazz Band ensembles all took high scores at the organizational competition. After the event's intense and unexpectedly great outcome with our scores and overall musicianship, Padawan ended up in tears (nearly giving all of the band members heart attacks!) and thanked us for such a wonderful year.

As wonderful as the season was, in concert, on the field, and at competitions in gymnasiums, everything good must end. We learned too well how much we take our band program for granted.

Mr. Padawan had a difficult choice to make for his family- one that eventually lead to a completely unexpected announcement after band one day in April, the day before our PSAE testing. Because he and his wife were expecting their first child over the summer, he had to make a decision about his job. On the average school day during the marching season, arriving at the school to open up the band room for us each morning at 7:30, he had an hour drive to school and an hour drive home after practice ended at 5:30 or 6:00. It was too much time wasted that he would need to spend with his family.

That day, few eyes were dry during sixth period in the band room. Mr. Padawan once again ended up with watery eyes as he announced his resignation. "I'm not leaving you guys for a better place, that's not it; I'm leaving for someplace different. It was such a hard decision to make… you guys are so fantastic; and this is hard, so hard to do."

We found out that day that flute players were definitely the biggest pansies of all the sections. In a cluster on the right side of the room, we huddled, sniffling, and I eventually had to pass around the few tissues I had in my purse.

What we also discovered, in the days to come, was how much change we would have to embrace as a group. There wouldn't be the band director who saved our program to pick out hard music for competition, hear us whine about it but improve gradually, and lead us into competition with the famous Padawan Pep-Talks.

In a leadership meeting several days later, he asked us to stick together no matter what. He picked our show, *Rise of the Machine*, so we would be able to prepare for our show during the transition period and run part of band camp with him, in order to keep up our newborn legacy of playing shows other bands wouldn't dare touch with a ten-foot pole. Both Zach and I made leadership team, and I was a bit bewildered, at first, about how we could possibly survive.

Later, when the crying was all done –and no one held it against our incredible band director- we formed a game plan and put everything in perspective.

We would survive, not as individuals, not as a leadership team alone, but as a band family. We've been in this situation before, although better prepared and given fair warning this time. We had risen from the ashes of the destruction of our former glory to become the machine that burns through dots and performs like we had nothing to lose on the field. All sections, different as they were, would stick together and perform; because on the field, we were not individuals, but parts of something greater.

Long live the Machine.

Acknowledgements

Many thanks are owed to those who helped make the season memorable and this book possible.

First, many thanks to Mr. Padawan, the Band director we all loved to pick on (just kidding!) for challenging us to become more than just individuals. Without you, we might never have seen a year this exciting and successful in our short time in high school. Thank you for making the year successful. We will miss you!

Thanks also goes to my parents, who read the chapters sleeplessly and proof-read without complaint: you believed I could write a book, and gave me all the support that I needed through the craziness. Lots of love!

To Brian, Maryn, Mat, and Levander- you guys rock for being so excited about each chapter. You helped motivate me to keep going when I thought I couldn't do it or when I considered giving up. Brian, thank you for the great photo.

Molly, Kayla, and Staci, you helped us have a successful year! Thank you for being so excited when I told you I was writing a book, and for allowing me to write about how awesome you were the whole season.

Many thanks to every band student who read a chapter (or a few!) and gave me advice. There are too many to mention by name, but I'm grateful for everyone's help!

Mrs. Woodward, I appreciate your assistance with this endeavor. You read many chapters of my rough draft. Thank you!

Dixie and Chuck, thank you for providing me with the tea that helped get the creative juices flowing when the ideas just wouldn't come to me and for the delightful interest in my writing.

Rachel, you were my pal throughout the season. Stay positive, Rachel!

To the band parents who fed us, clothed us, and supported us the whole way along our incredible journey: thank you for all your help to make such a wonderful season happen!

Mat, you kept me from taking my frustration out on my cranky printers and helped me put everything together. Thank you for deciphering all the computer mumbo-jumbo and explaining everything to me as many times as I needed. You're the best!

Zach, you are my tough "little" brother who won't admit that you read my book and actually liked it. It's because of you that I first began playing flute, and it's your fault I tried marching band. True story, bro. I'm glad I took both challenges. So, who won the bet?

ABOUT THE AUTHOR

Photo by Brian Munoz

Kaitlyn Auer is a 2013 graduate of Collinsville High School in Collinsville, Illinois. She became a band geek sixth grade after switching from choir to band when she was jealous of her brother's trumpet. She plays the flute and is completely awful at any other instrument, while her siblings can each play piano and various other instruments. But that doesn't bother her- her dream is to write and eventually become a best-selling author. She loves writing fiction, crocheting, painting, and is inspired most when drinking tea. She is currently working on craft books and plots for future novels.

www.ingramcontent.com/pod-product-compliance
Ingram Content Group UK Ltd.
Pitfield, Milton Keynes, MK11 3LW, UK
UKHW021051270726
13967UKWH00012B/573